Introduction

While baseball may be America's pastime, basketball is its passion. From driveways and playgrounds to gymnasiums and arenas, Americans' love affair with basketball is evident all over the country.

Maybe basketball's popularity has something to do with the simplicity of the game. Despite all of the complex plays and fancy moves that coaches and players have developed over the years, basketball remains simple.

For an official game, all you really need is one ball, two hoops, and ten players. The object is for one team of five players to put the ball into the hoop on their end of the court more times than the other team. It's really just a game of accuracy and basic math.

Yet it has become so much more. Thanks to top-notch high school, college, and professional teams, basketball has become one of the most popular sports in America. Some professional players gain the fame and fortune of movie stars or pop musicians. Kids and adults alike wear everything from hats to shoes that bear the names or symbols of their favorite players and teams. Basketball is a big business.

And it's spreading. With professional teams throughout Europe, Latin America, and Asia, basketball is popular all around the world.

But the frenzy and hype surrounding big-time basketball isn't really what the sport is about. It's about developing skills, staying fit, and learning teamwork. Most of all, it's about having fun. Let's go shoot some hoops.

Chapter 1

FROM SPRINGFIELD TO THE WORLD: A BRIEF HISTORY OF BASKETBALL

It might be hard to believe, but basketball hasn't been around all that long. In fact, people were playing such sports as soccer, baseball, football, golf, and tennis long before basketball.

Dr. James Naismith invented the game in the winter of 1891. He was teaching a gym class for Springfield College in Springfield, Massachusetts, and the young men in the class were bored with marching and calisthenics. Naismith tried outdoor games such as football and soccer in the YMCA gymnasium where his class met, but neither sport worked well in the cramped space. He realized that what he needed was a game that combined some of the skills and benefits of football, rugby, and lacrosse, but could be played in a gym.

Then Naismith remembered a game he'd liked as a boy growing up in Ontario, Canada, called Duck on a Rock. He and his friends had tried to knock a small rock off the top of a boulder by throwing other rocks at it. While some players had pitched their rocks hard and straight, the most successful ones had lobbed their rocks in an arc toward the target.

That gave Naismith the idea for a game in which

Dr. James Naismith, founder of Basketball. (Courtesy of Naismith Memorial Basketball Hall of Fame.)

players tossed a ball at some sort of goal. His first idea for a goal was a box, but when the YMCA didn't have any on hand, he settled for a pair of peach baskets that were stored in the basement.

BASKETS TO HOOPS

Standing on a ladder, Naismith nailed one basket to the side of a balcony at one end of the gym. Then he nailed the other basket to the side of a balcony at the opposite end. Both baskets were ten feet off the floor, the same height as basketball goals today.

Before his students could play the game, Naismith knew he had to have some rules. So, a few minutes before trying basketball out on his class, he sat down with a pad of paper and a pencil and wrote down thirteen rules for the new sport. Most of them were similar to the rules we have today. For instance: "A player cannot run with the ball." And: "A goal shall be made when the ball is thrown or batted from the grounds into the basket. . . ." And, of course: "The side making the most goals in [the game] shall be declared the winners."

After his secretary hurriedly typed up the list, Naismith thumbtacked it to a bulletin board inside the gym. Then he picked up a soccer ball, divided his class of eighteen students into two teams of nine, and the signaled the start of the world's first basketball game. It wasn't much like the fast-paced game of today. In fact, only one player managed to make a basket. The final score was 1–0.

But even as the students got more confidence on the court, games were slow. For one thing, Naismith hadn't cut out the bottoms of the baskets. If a player actually got the soccer ball into a goal, the game had to stop while someone fished it out. Sometimes that was as simple as having a person in the balcony lean over the railing, pull the ball out, and toss it back down to the floor. Other times, Naismith would climb a ladder to get the ball. Fortunately, in the early games players spent more time scrambling around after the ball than they did making baskets.

The baskets continued to have bottoms in them for several years, even after the game became widespread. As a few companies began making baskets for the new sport, they devised ways to get the ball out; one company attached a chain to the basket so a player or referee could pull it to open the bottom of the basket and let the ball fall out. Finally, someone came up with the idea of using just an metal hoop with a net hanging from it. That's the design we use today. (But when we score, we still say we "made a basket"!)

Even though baskets had no nets at the time, Naismith first called his new game "netball." One of his students suggested "Naismith ball," but he only laughed. When the same student suggested calling the game "basket-ball" because they were trying to shoot a ball into a peach basket, Naismith agreed. Basketball it was—and still is.

THE EARLY YEARS

Word spread rapidly that the students in Naismith's class were having a good time playing the new game he'd invented. As the game caught on among students, interest in it quickly followed, with people eager to both try it out and see it played.

In fact, the first public basketball game was played on

March 12, 1892, in the Springfield YMCA. It was game between Naismith's students and teachers from Springfield College, with two hundred people watching. The final score was 5–1 in favor of the students.

Because Naismith's first basketball games were played inside a YMCA gymnasium, other Y's around the country heard about the new sport soon after its invention. And with Naismith's help, basketball quickly became part of YMCA schedules nationwide, especially after a survey revealed that the sport was attracting new members to the organization.

In addition to the YMCA, athletic clubs around the country added basketball to their programs. Overseen by the Amateur Athletic Union (the AAU), many of these clubs organized teams and began competing against one another. Church leagues also sprang up quickly. By 1897 there was a church-sponsored team in New York, and seven years later the city was home to a league of church-sponsored teams. Large factories and businesses formed teams, as did the U.S. Army and Navy, and American Indian reservations.

As America celebrated the arrival of the twentieth century, basketball had earned a place among the nation's most popular sports.

A Changing Game

As it spread, basketball began to change. For instance, the pivot was introduced in 1893. One of Naismith's original thirteen rules prevented a player with the ball from doing anything except passing or shooting it. But the pivot changed that.

Instead of simply standing still, a player with the ball could turn on one foot, which helped keep the ball away from defenders. It also allowed a player to catch a pass while facing away from the basket, then turn and take a shot.

In the beginning of the game, there was no foul line. In his original thirteen rules, Naismith had stated that three fouls by players on one team would automatically result in a point for the other team. A foul, said Naismith, would be called on a player who hit the ball with a fist, or shouldered, hit, tripped, pushed, or struck an opposing player.

By 1894 Naismith and others involved with the sport agreed that there ought to be another type of penalty for players who committed a foul—that is, pushed, bumped, hit, or had some other physical contact with an opponent. The *free throw* (or *foul shot*) was born: that's an un-guarded shot taken by the player on whom the foul was committed. With free throws came the *free throw line* (or *foul line*), which was set at fifteen feet from each basket, the same distance it is today.

Early basketball games were played wherever there was enough room—in gymnasiums, of course, but also in dance halls, armories, and auditoriums. Anywhere with enough floor space would do. The first courts were small: fifty feet long and thirty-five feet wide. Compare that to courts today: college and professional teams, as well as most high school teams, play on courts that are ninety-four feet long and fifty feet wide. Every so often a game was played outside.

Not only were most early courts small, but they were also bare. There were no markings on them until the foul line was introduced. It wasn't until 1932 that the next

Game and equipment as used in 1892. (From lecture material of Amos Alonzo Stagg. Courtesy of Naismith Memorial Basketball Hall of Fame.)

mark appeared: the *midcourt line,* which is the line that runs side to side across the middle of the court, dividing it into two equal halves. It came with the introduction of the ten-second rule, which is still in effect. This rule says that, after one team has scored a basket, the other team has ten seconds from the time one of its players inbounds the ball from behind the opponent's basket to get it across the midcourt line, or lose possession.

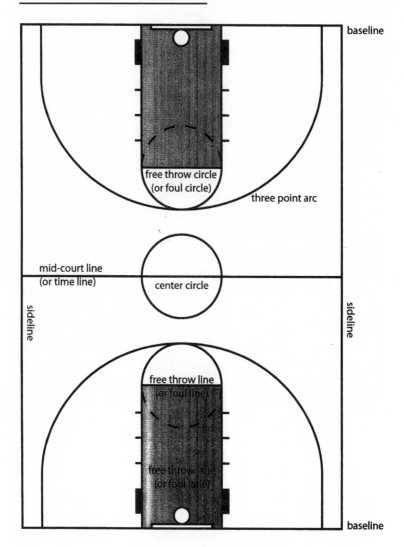

Today's basketball court

As the game evolved, other markings were added. Now there are *baselines,* which mark the two ends of the court, and *sidelines,* which mark the sides. There's the *center circle,* which is where the game-opening tip-off (or jump ball) takes place. There are *free throw lanes* (or *foul lanes*) in front of the baskets; marked at each end by a free throw line and a baseline, the lane marks an area into which no player can step when someone is shooting a free throw. Finally, there are the *three-point arcs,* curved lines at each end of the court. Baskets scored by players standing behind the arc are worth three points, rather than the two points that baskets in front of the arcs are worth. With all of their markings, today's courts look like abstract paintings.

For the first couple of years after Naismith invented the sport, "basketball" continued to be played with soccer balls (brown leather ones rather than the white rubber ones we're used to today). It wasn't until 1894 that the Overman Wheel Company in Chicopee Falls, Massachusetts, developed a bigger ball for use on the court. Though made of leather and sewn together with thick laces that made it hard to bounce, the new basketball was similar in size and weight to today's balls (which are nine inches in diameter and weigh twenty-two ounces when fully inflated).

In 1928 the first concealed-lace ball debuted: the laces, which held the two halves of the leather ball together, were tucked neatly out of the way under a flap, resulting in a smoother, better-bouncing surface. It was in the 1940s that ball manufacturers developed the technology that allowed them to pour hot, liquid rubber into molds, fusing two halves together to create a seamless ball. Using molten rubber also allowed them to experiment with colors. Basketballs, which were long available mostly in shades of brown, could be made in various colors. Today you can walk into any sporting goods store and find not only brown basketballs, but balls in an array of hues as well, from the red-white-and-blue balls of the American Basketball Association (ABA) to balls bearing the colors of various college and professional teams.

Then there's the matter of players' uniforms. Early on, players wore an assortment of clothes on the court, ranging from knickers and long-sleeved shirts to track suits (which looked a lot like long underwear) or itchy, woolen football uniforms (minus the pads). Their shoes were anything from rubber-soled gym shoes to leather-soled street shoes. It wasn't until 1903 that the Spalding Company first made canvas basketball shoes with special rubber suction soles that were supposed to be slip-proof on any type of floor. They ranged in price from $1 to $4 a pair—a lot cheaper than today's high-tech, flashy shoes that range in price from $50 to $150 a pair.

As basketball gained popularity and organized teams were developed, uniforms became—well, uniform. At first, they were sort of modified long johns, but gradually they began to move toward the jerseys and shorts we're familiar with today. The biggest change in recent years has been the move from the shorter shorts favored by players in the 1950s, '60s, and '70s to the long, baggy shorts that are standard on high school, college, and professional courts of the twenty-first century.

Another issue that affected basketball in its early years was rowdy fans. How rowdy were they? Rowdy enough that courts often were surrounded by metal fences or wire or cloth netting. This was not only to keep the ball on the court, but also to protect the players from

The Armory cage in Paterson, New Jersey, site of the American Basketball League Games, 1919–1933. (Courtesy of Naismith Memorial Basketball Hall of Fame.)

the folks in the stands. Playing in these "cages" is how basketball players earned the nickname cagers.

But while the thick wire protected them from spectators, it injured players, too: opponents often slammed one another into the wire. It was like being bodychecked into the boards in hockey, only without the protective padding. Imagine trying to play basketball after someone has rammed you into a fence!

By the 1920s the caged courts began to disappear—perhaps because players preferred to take their chances with the fans than with the fencing. There were plenty of fans by then—and plenty of players. Today the closest thing we have to the old caged courts are fenced outdoor courts, which show up mostly in large cities or on university campuses. But even where they're present, the courts are usually large enough that the fences are set back from the baselines and sidelines, which protects players from having fence patterns imprinted on their faces.

Balconies to Backboards

Following Naismith's lead, early basketball teams often hung their baskets from gym balconies. The only problem with this was that people sitting in balcony seats could reach over the railing and either block shots or guide them into the basket.

The solution was the backboard. Introduced in 1895, the backboard provided a flat surface to which a basket could be attached. Then the backboard could be mounted on a pole or a wall, preventing spectators from interfering with players' shots.

B-BALL GOES TO COLLEGE

Within a few months of the game's invention, colleges and universities began to add basketball to their physical education programs. Both Geneva College in Pennsylvania and the University of Iowa had men's basketball programs by 1892. But it was University of Toronto in Canada that became the first college team to play basketball against an outside team. In January 1893 a university-sponsored men's team played a team from the Toronto YMCA. The university team won the game 2–1.

The first game between two college teams was a Yale University versus University of Pennsylvania contest in March 1897. It was the first college-level game in which the two teams agreed to limit the number of players on the floor to five for each team; that later became the official standard, the one that's still in use today. Yale came out on top with a score of 32–10.

One problem for the first few colleges and universities that formed basketball teams was the lack of competition. As a result, the college-level teams that existed often had to play games against whomever they could find—teams from local YMCAs, high schools, churches, and so forth. With little experience, college teams sometimes found themselves losing games to much younger (but better) opponents.

By the early 1900s, however, basketball had become an accepted part of college athletic programs nationwide. That led to the creation of leagues and conferences— teams from schools that are similar in size or located close enough to each other to play against one another. Among the earliest were the Eastern League (which is now the Ivy League), the Western Conference (now the Big Ten Conference), and the New England League (which no longer exists).

As the sport grew in popularity on American campuses, it attracted large crowds of spectators. Those large crowds, in turn, led to the construction of larger gymnasiums and field houses—the predecessors of the huge arenas that are found on many campuses today.

Naturally, once colleges and universities had created leagues and conferences, and built gyms and field houses, the basketball coaches wanted to test their teams against others around the country. The result was the creation of basketball tournaments.

One of the earliest tournaments was played in 1908, with the Eastern League's champions, the University of Pennsylvania, facing the Western Conference champions, the University of Chicago. Fired by the hot hands of guard Pat Page, the University of Chicago won the best-of-three series in two straight. In the first game, Page hit a miraculous under-the-legs shot for a 21–18 win, while in the second game he led a charge that resulted in a 16–15 victory. Exciting games like these attracted a lot of attention, increased public interest in the game, and ensured the future of college tournaments.

In 1938 the first National Invitational Tournament (NIT) was held in New York's Madison Square Garden. Conceived by a New York sportswriter named Edward "Ned" Irish and sponsored by the Metropolitan Basketball Writers Association, the NIT was promoted as the "Rose Bowl of Basketball." It featured teams from New York, Pennsylvania, Colorado, and Oklahoma, and attracted huge crowds. In the end, Temple University walked away with the first-ever NIT trophy after drubbing the University of Colorado 60–36.

That merely set the stage for the second NIT event, which featured the first (and last) matchup between two unbeaten college teams in a national tournament. The teams were Long Island University from New York and Loyola College from Chicago. One of the Long Island players, Mike Sewich, played the game with a broken arm but still managed to shut down Loyola's top scorer, which helped LIU win the 1939 NIT title.

Today the NIT is still held in Madison Square Garden, having grown to a thirty-two-team competition. Now under the direction of the Metropolitan Intercollegiate Basketball Association, a New York–based organization consisting of Fordham University, Manhattan College, New York University, St. John's University, and Wagner College, the tournament's lineup is chosen each year by representatives from the five MIBA schools.

While it was once the premier postseason event for men's college basketball, however, the NIT has lost its crown to a higher-profile tournament: the National Collegiate Athletic Association (NCAA) Tournament. The NCAA, which has headquarters in Indianapolis, Indiana, was started in 1906. It oversees collegiate sports programs, including basketball programs, run by the more than a thousand public, private, and religious universities and colleges that are NCAA members. The annual basketball tournament is one of the NCAA's biggest, most famous events.

Held in March every year, the NCAA Tournament, which also is known as the Big Dance, was first held in 1939. It featured four teams from four geographic regions in the United States and was held on the campus of Northwestern University in Evanston, Illinois. After the initial semifinals, the first-ever NCAA basketball championship game pitted the Tall Timbers of the University of Oregon against the Buckeyes of Ohio State University. Oregon won, 46–33.

Though not as well attended or as widely promoted as the NIT in New York, the 1939 NCAA Tournament laid the foundation for what was to come. Today, it's the NCAA event rather than the NIT that university and college coaches dream of attending. In fact, the NIT is sometimes viewed as a consolation prize: the thirty-two teams that take part in that tournament are chosen from among a large pool of teams that don't make the NCAA Tournament's sixty-four-team roster.

The NCAA Tournament involves the top sixty-four Division I men's teams in the country. Division I is one of three categories that the NCAA uses for its members' athletic programs. There are also Divisions II and III. Division I schools are colleges and universities that have at least seven sports for men and seven for women. Because of the expense of sponsoring so many sports, Division I consists primarily of large schools with large athletic program budgets.

(Division II schools have to have at least four sports for men and four for women, with at least two team sports for each gender. They tend to be medium-sized schools, with many of their student-athletes coming from the communities in which the schools are located. Division III schools have to have at least five sports for men and five for women, with none of their athletes receiving sports-related scholarships. They tend to be small community or private colleges.)

As the tournament progresses, teams are eliminated in regional competitions (Southeast, West, East, and Midwest). By the last weekend only four teams are left, one from each of the four geographic regions. Known as the Final Four, it pits the four regional winners against one another, with the winner of the final game being crowned NCAA champion—which, to many basketball fans, means "the best college team in the country."

The NCAA Tournament is one of the most popular basketball events in the country. College students skip classes and adults leave work early just to watch tournament games on television—or if they're fortunate enough to get tickets, attend them in person. Because it generates so much excitement among fans across the country, the NCAA Tournament is the cause for an annual outbreak of "March Madness."

In addition to the NCAA Tournament and the NIT, the National Association of Intercollegiate Athletics (NAIA), which is based in Olathe, Kansas, also plays host to a thirty-two-team tournament every year. Like the NCAA, the NAIA oversees sports programs at a variety of colleges and universities (about five hundred of them), most of which are much smaller in enrollment and in number of sports programs than NCAA schools. The NAIA's annual thirty-two-team college men's basketball tournament takes place in Kansas City, and provides NAIA member teams a chance to compete in a national arena, though admittedly without much of the hoopla that surrounds the NCAA event.

While tournaments allow star players to light up the courts and make headlines, some of the best-known stars of college basketball are the coaches. Throughout the history of the sport, innovative, inspiring college coaches have become legends. One of the most legendary was the father of basketball himself: James Naismith moved to Lawrence, Kansas, in 1899 to become the coach of the men's varsity basketball team at the University of Kansas. He held the position for ten years.

Strangely enough, Naismith believed that while basketball skills could be taught, the game itself could not be coached, which is why he held only sporadic practice sessions and almost never attended games, whether at home or away. When he did go to a game, he usually acted as a referee, never bothering to develop game plans or strategies for his players. To Naismith, the point of basketball was to get some exercise: he didn't care about winning games or tournament titles. And he didn't care about coaching.

But plenty of his successors have. In fact, one of the best-known college coaches from the past was a friend and former student of Naismith's—Forrest "Phog" Allen. He coached the University of Kansas team from 1920 to 1956, winning 746 games, twenty-four conference titles, and the 1952 NCAA tournament trophy in the process. Allen's attitude about coaching was the exact opposite of Naismith's: Allen considered basketball a competitive game to be studied and mastered. Naismith, in turn, served as his assistant for many years, even though the two men disagreed about the purpose of the sport.

One of Allen's players, in turn, went on to become a coaching legend himself—Adolph Rupp, who led the University of Kentucky Wildcats from 1931 to 1972, winning 876 games along the way. Rupp, who was once the winningest coach of all time, lost the title to another legend—Dean Smith, who headed up the University of

North Carolina's basketball team from 1962 to 1997, tallied 879 games. The most famous player to come out of Smith's program was Michael Jordan, who credited Smith with teaching him many valuable lessons.

Among other great college basketball coaches worth learning about are Denny Crum (who took over the University of Kentucky coaching duties from Rupp); Nat Holman (City College of New York); John Wooden (UCLA); Digger Phelps (Notre Dame University); Branch McCracken and Bobby Knight (both Indiana University); Gene Keady (Purdue University); John Thompson (Georgetown University); and Mike Krzyzewski (Duke University). Many of these figures have written books, or have had books written about them, that offer good insights into what coaching basketball is all about.

Successful, well-known coaches are at the heart of college basketball. A good coach is able to recruit good players, and good players generate excitement about a team. That's a source of pride for students, faculty, and alumni. But there's more to it than that. While players graduate and move on, a coach whose teams do well continues to be an asset to the school, attracting press coverage and enticing people to buy tickets to games. In fact, a big-name basketball coach is a leading source of income for college and university athletic departments, thanks not only to ticket sales but also to lucrative radio and television broadcasting deals, endorsement contracts from sports equipment, shoe, and apparel companies, and advertising revenue from businesses eager to get their names seen by fans attending games or watching them on television.

NOT JUST A GUY THING

Just weeks after Naismith's gym class began playing basketball, a group of female teachers from the nearby Buckingham Grade School walked past the Springfield YMCA on their way to lunch. Attracted by the noise coming from inside the gym, the women peeked through an open door and saw a basketball game in progress.

That was all it took. After watching for a while, they asked Naismith to teach them how to play. When he did, they took the sport back to their school and taught it to their elementary school students. One of those teachers was Maude Sherman, who eventually married James Naismith.

Basketball has never been a sport just for guys. Naismith never meant for it to be. In 1892 he helped organize the first women's team at the Springfield YMCA, which included some of the teachers from Buckingham. The following year Naismith met Senda Berenson at a convention for physical education instructors. After learning about basketball from him, she introduced the sport to her students at Smith College, an all-female school in Northampton, Massachusetts. Her enthusiasm for the game, and her dedication to it over many years, eventually earned her the title of the Mother of Basketball. (Guess who was the Father.)

By 1895 several other women's colleges were teaching the sport. That led Clara Gregory Baer, a physical education instructor at Sophie Newcomb College in New Orleans, to write the first list of rules for women's basketball. Though similar to the rules for men, Baer's contained some changes. For instance, she divided the court into three sections, and required players to stay in one of the sections throughout the game—they couldn't run up and down the length of the court. In 1938 the three-section court was reduced to two sections, separated by the mid-court line, but the players were still assigned to one half of the court or the other, and couldn't move back and forth as they do today.

Women also had to put up with a lot more officiating than men in the early days. There were as many as eleven officials on the court during some women's games, which must have made it pretty crowded out there. Today there are only two referees on the court, which is much more manageable.

The number of players in women's games varied widely. In the 1920s women's teams were allowed to have between five and ten players each on the floor at a time. By the 1930s the number was fixed at six players, which is where it remained until the 1970s when women's basketball adopted the men's on-the-floor rule of five players per team.

Today the differences between men's and women's basketball are much less drastic than in the past. While women now play a full-court game and move freely around the floor just as men do, they use a ball that is an inch smaller and two and a half ounces lighter than the men's. On the professional level, women's teams have thirty seconds in which to take a shot, while men have twenty-four (but on the college level, women still have thirty seconds, while men have thirty-five). The foul lane for women (college and professional) is only twelve feet wide, while for professional men it's nineteen feet. There are a few other differences, but they're all minor. For the most part, basketball is played the same way today regardless of gender.

Like men, women had to put up with ridiculous clothing in the sport's early days. At first, women were
required to wear long dresses when they played basketball—until they got tired of tripping over the hems whenever they tried to move around on the court. That led, in
1896, to the introduction of "bloomers." Basically knee-
length pants that puffed out (bloomed), they were worn
with long stockings. By the 1920s bloomers had given
way to short-sleeved tops and knee-length skirts, which
were replaced in the 1930s by shorts and sleeveless tops.
Women players have worn variations on these outfits
ever since.

From the beginning, women's basketball was popular
all across the country. As with the men's version, it
spread rapidly among colleges and universities. On April
4, 1896, Stanford University and the University of
California played the first women's basketball game between two colleges. Stanford won the low-scoring game
by the narrow margin of 2–1.

One of the first women's team to gain international
fame was the Edmonton Grads, which was formed in
Edmonton, a city in the Canadian province of Alberta, in
1915. Made up originally of graduates of the McDougal
Commercial High School in Edmonton, the team at-
tracted attention first when it defeated the London
Shamrock, a women's team from London, Ontario, in the
Canadian equivalent of the NCAA Tournament.

Then, in 1923, the Grads were invited to take part in
the first Underwood Trophy Series, sponsored by the
Underwood Typewriter Company. In that competition
the Grads, dressed in out-of-fashion bloomers and long
woolen stockings, defeated the Cleveland Favorite Knits,
whose members wore tight-fitting jerseys and shorts

bearing the words WORLD CHAMPS. That was a title that was awarded to the Grads after the game. From that point until the team disbanded in 1940, the Grads tallied a respectable 114 wins and 6 losses!

In 1926 the first National Women's Basketball Championship was held. Organized by the Amateur Athletic Union (AAU), the tournament became a symbol of the importance of basketball among young women nationwide. In 1931 one of basketball's first female stars emerged when Babe Didrikson racked up more than twenty points per game in the AAU championship competition. The team she played for—the Golden Cyclones from Dallas, Texas—won the championship. And Didrikson went on to win gold medals in javelin throwing and hurdles at the 1932 Olympics, then to further fame as a professional golfer.

Just three years after Didrikson's Olympic triumphs the All-American Redheads were formed in Cassville, Missouri. It was a women's team made entirely of redheads (most of whom depended on hair coloring for their red hair). Starting with some naturally talented Missouri players, team owner C. M. "Ole" Olson recruited AAU All-Americans as well, then urged them not only to play good basketball, but to add some tricks to their playing skills as well. In the process, the All-American Redheads became the female version of the Harlem Globetrotters, traveling the world to promote women's basketball.

Over the fifty-year life of the team (1936 to 1986), its player list included such stars as Lorene "Butch" Moore, who scored more than thirty-five thousand points over an eleven-year career. She could do such amazing on-court feats as bouncing the ball off her head while driving in for a layup—and making the basket! She also kneeled at the free throw line during halftime and made twenty-five consecutive free throws. With a player such as Moore on board, the Redheads earned a reputation for putting on a great show, while showcasing just how good women could be on the basketball court.

The Redheads' success led to the formation of other women's traveling teams. With names such as the Arkansas Travelers, the Texas Cowgirls, and the Bonnie Wee Lassies, the teams gave talented women players a chance to make some money and have some fun at a time when there weren't many opportunities for female athletes to use their skills professionally.

In 1971 the Association of Intercollegiate Athletics for Women (AIAW) made its debut. During its twelve-year history (1971 to 1983), it was responsible for organizing tournaments in all types of college women's sports, including basketball. The AIAW also got involved in efforts to get Title IX passed by Congress. Part of the Educational Amendments of 1972, Title IX called for equal treatment of women and men in educational settings such as colleges and universities. When Congress passed Title IX, women athletes gained the right to have the same access as men to sports programs in their schools. One sport that boomed as a result was women's basketball.

Consequently, in 1981 the NCAA added a women's basketball tournament to its March roster. Just as in the men's competition, the number of teams in the annual NCAA women's basketball tournament is gradually whittled down in four regional champions. The four winners then compete for the tournament title in their own Final Four. As in the men's tournament, the one team left at the end of the single-elimination competition (lose a game and your team's out) is crowned champion.

The NCCA women's basketball tournament got a real boost in 1995. That was the year that the University of Connecticut's women's basketball team, led by star player Rebecca Lobo, not only went undefeated in the regular season (35–0) but also went on to win every game it played in the NCAA women's tournament. Connecticut's success made even doubters realize the high level of play taking place in women's basketball. As a result, the women's tournament has become so popular that getting tickets to its Final Four games is just as difficult as getting them for the men's tournament. March Madness is an equal opportunity affliction.

Unfortunately, one of the by-products of the growth of women's basketball at NCAA member schools was the death of the AIAW. As women's athletic programs gained stature and status within NCAA colleges and universities, their coaches and athletes got involved with NCAA programs; as a result, AIAW membership dropped off. Finally, in 1983, the organization called it quits; but by then its place in sports history as a pioneer in the effort to popularize college women's basketball was assured.

Today women's college basketball programs are popular throughout the United States. From local state colleges to nationally known universities, basketball fans show up in droves to support their favorite teams. According to statistics compiled by the University of Wisconsin—Madison Women's Sports Information Office, NCAA Division I women's basketball teams attracted more than three million fans to home games during the 2000–2001 season. That number isn't likely to decrease anytime soon.

B-BALL GOES TO HIGH SCHOOL

High schools also caught the basketball bug early. The first boys' high school league in the country was in Denver, Colorado, in 1896. It was started by none other than James Naismith, who had moved from Massachusetts to Colorado to be the physical education director at the Denver YMCA—and to attend medical school, which is what eventually earned him the nickname Doc. Because none of the schools in Denver had gymnasiums equipped for the sport, the teams played their games at the Y where Naismith worked.

Basketball was still new at the time, so it was up to Naismith to teach Denver's high school players how to play the sport. He also acted as the referee for their games. Imagine learning to play basketball from the guy who invented it—then having him referee your games!

The first basketball game between two high schools took place in 1897 when Holyoke High School in Holyoke, Massachusetts, defeated Philadelphia Central High School from Philadelphia, Pennsylvania. And the first statewide high school tournament took place in Appleton, Wisconsin, in 1905.

But the most famous high school game in basketball history took place in 1954, at Butler Fieldhouse on the campus of Butler University in Indianapolis. It was the final game in the Indiana State High School Basketball Championships, and it pitted Muncie Central, a powerhouse city team, against Milan High School, a tiny rural school team.

With eighteen seconds left in the game, the score was tied 30–30. After a brief time-out, Milan threw the ball inbounds and passed it around. With five seconds left, the ball went to Milan's star shooter, Bobby Plump. When he started to drive for the basket, his defender eased off, and Plump stopped and took a jump shot that went in at the buzzer! Milan won the state title 32–30.

That game was the inspiration, years later, for one of the most popular basketball movies ever made— *Hoosiers*. In fact, Indiana has perhaps the most devoted high school basketball fans in the United States. Kids in Indiana grow up surrounded by basketball: there are hoops in nearly every park and on nearly every school playground. The largest gymnasium in the world is at New Castle High School in New Castle, Indiana.

New Castle is also the home of the Indiana Basketball Hall of Fame, which memorializes the state's b-ball legends and proves that Indiana has produced some of basketball's finest players. Oscar Robertson, George McGinnis, Billy Keller, Larry Bird, and Steve Alford are among the hundreds of former players who've been honored by the Indiana Basketball Hall of Fame.

Of course, Indiana isn't the only place where basketball is big. In fact, finding a high school anywhere in America that doesn't have a basketball team (or a gym to play in) would be hard today. High school basketball for both boys and girls is popular nationwide, with an estimated one million students playing on school teams every year—and millions more playing on intramural teams.

BASKETBALL IN THE OLYMPICS

Basketball was added to the Olympic Games in 1904, but only as a demonstration sport. It wasn't until 1936 that basketball became an official Olympic sport, making its debut that year at the games in Berlin, Germany. What that debut revealed was how popular basketball had become around the world. More countries sent teams to compete in basketball than in any other sport in the 1936 Olympics.

During that competition, the United States won the first-ever gold medal in the sport, defeating a team from Canada 19–8 on a muddy, outdoor tennis court. One American player, six-foot, eight-inch center Joe Fortenberry, matched Canada's team total by scoring eight points of his own!

World War II led to a twelve-year gap in Olympic competitions, but when they resumed in London, England, in 1948, the American team again dominated basketball, winning the gold medal. But four years later, when the USSR sent its first postwar basketball team to compete, it created a rivalry with the Americans that lasted until the collapse of the Soviet Union in 1989. Of course, the rivalry on court only reflected the political rivalry between the United States and the USSR: this was the era of the Cold War, when tensions ran high between the two countries. Sports competitions were a way for those tensions to be acted upon without war breaking out.

The basketball rivalry led the U.S. team to defeat the Soviets for the Olympic gold medal in 1952, 1956, 1960, 1964, and 1976. But the United States lost the gold-medal game in 1972 in the most controversial outcome in Olympic basketball history.

By the time they reached the 1972 finals, both the U.S. and the Soviet teams were undefeated in the preliminary rounds. They played a hard-fought game, and with three seconds remaining the USSR was ahead 49–48. But American player Doug Collins was fouled, and he sank two free throws, putting the Americans in the lead 50–49.

Though the Soviets had possession of the ball, they failed to score before time ran out. Everyone in the arena where the game was being played thought it was over. The American team began to celebrate. But confusion over a horn that had sounded before the clock ran out led officials to order the clock reset, and the final three seconds to be replayed.

Given another chance, the Soviets didn't connect on a long pass, the clock ran out, and again the Americans thought they had won. But a high-ranking Olympics official said no, claiming that the clock hadn't been properly reset before the referees had allowed play to begin. So the clock was set at three seconds one more time. This time the Soviets managed to get the ball to a player who scored as time ran out—for the third time—and the USSR was declared the gold-medal winner. In protest, the Americans refused to accept their silver medals.

Despite such disappointments, American men's teams have dominated Olympic basketball competitions, due to the quality of the players they have consistently been able to put on the floor. Over the years America's Olympic roster has included such basketball greats as Bill Russell, Oscar Robinson, Jerry Lucas, Jerry West, Bill Bradley, Spencer Haywood, Quinn Buckner, Chris Mullen, Patrick Ewing, David Robinson, Larry Bird, Clyde Drexler, John Stockton, Christian Laettner, Grant Hill, Reggie Miller, Vince Carter, Ray Allen, and Kevin Garnett.

Women's basketball hasn't been an Olympic sport nearly as long. It wasn't until the 1976 Olympics in Montreal that the first women's basketball competition took place. Since then, American women's teams have brought home four gold medals—in 1984, 1988, 1996, and 2000.

Like the men's team, the American women's Olympic roster has attracted the country's top female talent. Among the outstanding players who have competed for the U.S. team have been Nancy Lieberman, Cheryl Miller, Lynette Woodard, Teresa Edwards, Katrina McClain, Cynthia Cooper, Medina Dixon, Lisa Leslie, Ruthie Bolton, Sheryl Swoopes, Yolanda Griffith, Teresa Weatherspoon, and Rebecca Lobo.

Starting in 1995, USA Basketball, the organization that's officially in charge of the training and development of the American men's and women's basketball teams for the Olympics, has allowed the women's team to train for an entire year before an Olympics competition. That allows the best players to work together under the guidance of the coach who will be with them at the Olympics.

The first women's team to do this was the one chosen to represent the United States at the 1996 Olympics. To prepare, the team played fifty-two games against American college teams and teams abroad. It won all fifty-two—a sign of the Olympic victories to come. At the Olympic competition in Atlanta in 1996, the U.S. women's team went undefeated, winning the gold medal and attracting crowds in excess of thirty thousand in the process.

THE DREAM TEAM ELEVATES THE GAME

The worldwide passion for basketball really took off after a rule barring professional players from competing in Olympics was changed. That led to the creation of the

Dream Team, which represented the United States in the men's basketball competition in the 1992 Olympic Games in Barcelona, Spain.

Featuring NBA stars such as Michael Jordan, Magic Johnson, and Larry Bird, the Dream Team rolled over the teams from other countries, winning a gold medal and elevating basketball's status internationally. That status remains high today: the only sport that's more popular worldwide than basketball is soccer. This seems ironic when you consider the fact that James Naismith's first basketball was a soccer ball!

The Original Dream Team

The first U.S. Olympic men's basketball team to be called the Dream Team was the 1992 squad led by Larry Bird, Magic Johnson, and Michael Jordan. But many basketball fans and historians point to the 1960 American team as the original dream team.

That's because the 1960 team included such soon-to-be NBA legends as Oscar Robertson and Jerry West, a pair of guards who were two of basketball's all-time great shooters. Joining them were such other rising stars as Jerry Lucas, Walt Bellamy, Bob Boozer, and Terry Dischinger.

This American team not only won the gold medal in the 1960 Olympics, but did so by sweeping all of its opponents with a game-winning average of more than forty-two points. It was also the same team that was first to gain international fame—because the 1960 Olympic Games were the first to be televised worldwide.

Chapter 2

B-BALL GOES TO WORK: PROFESSIONAL BASKETBALL, PAST AND PRESENT

The National Basketball Association (NBA) is more than the top-level professional basketball organization in North America—it's the top-level professional basketball organization in the world. From its headquarters in New York, the NBA oversees not only its own twenty-nine-team league in North America, but also offices in Europe, Japan, China, and Australia. Professional basketball is a big business all over the globe.

That hasn't always been true. The first professional basketball game on record took place in Trenton, New Jersey, in 1896. A group of guys who'd been playing at the local YMCA rented a dance hall, installed a couple of baskets, and charged people to watch them play. They weren't trying to get rich—they just wanted to get back the money they'd spent renting the hall.

But so many people showed up that the players not only covered the rental fee, they each earned fifteen dollars in profit—with one exception. The guy who'd organized the game took home sixteen bucks, which made him professional basketball's first highest-paid player.

In 1898 the National Basketball League was organized in Philadelphia, with teams in that city and in nearby New Jersey. It was the first of many professional leagues to come: some lasted a few months, others a few years. Players often played for more than one league at a time, using different names in each league.

One of the first professional leagues to do well was the American Basketball League, which operated from 1925 to 1931. The ABL, which had teams in major cities throughout the country, was the first league to offer players exclusive contracts. Unfortunately, the Great Depression led to hard times for the league, and the ABL was forced out of business.

It was followed by the National Basketball League, which was formed in 1937. With the financial backing of several large companies, it hired the best players around. But because its teams were mostly in small cities and played in small arenas, it never made much money. While its star players made big salaries for the time (up to sixty thousand dollars), the NBL struggled to stay in business.

THE NBA EMERGES

It wasn't until the formation of the Basketball Association of America (BAA) in 1946 that professional basketball as we know it began to take shape. The BAA was created by the owners of arenas and hockey teams in New York, Boston, Philadelphia, Cleveland, St. Louis, Chicago, Providence, Pittsburgh, Toronto, and Washington, D.C., who were looking for another way to make money. Basketball seemed to fit the bill.

The BAA kicked off its first season on November 1, 1946, with a game between the New York Knickerbockers and the Toronto Huskies, in Toronto. As a Canadian city, Toronto was more familiar with hockey than basketball: whenever a referee called for a jump ball, people in the stands would yell, "Face-off!" And the crowd of ten thousand applauded politely whenever either team scored. Maybe that's why it was a close game: the Knicks barely squeaked past the Huskies 68–66.

When New York played its first home game at Madison Square Garden a few days later, a crowd of seventeen thousand fans showed up. Unlike the Toronto folks, the New York crowd was rowdy, hooting and clapping throughout the game. With many of the Knicks being former stars on local college teams, they were seen as hometown boys, and the crowd cheered them on. New York was a basketball town, and it loved the Knicks from the beginning.

The first true BAA star was "Jumpin' Joe" Fulks, a six foot, five-inch forward who gained fame for his two-handed, overhead jump shot. Playing for the Philadelphia Warriors, Fulks scored twenty-five points in his (and his team's) first professional game in 1946 using his famous "ear shot," so called because he pulled the ball back beside his right ear before releasing it. Using his unusual shot and his uncanny ability to score almost at will, he tossed in an astounding sixty-three points in a game against the Indianapolis Jets in 1949.

When the National Basketball League finally collapsed that same year, ten of its teams joined the BAA, and the league was renamed the National Basketball Association. The NBA era had begun. Three of the original BAA teams are still part of the NBA today: the Knicks, the Boston Celtics, and the Golden State Warriors (which were originally the Philadelphia Warriors).

Along with Fulks, one of the NBA's early crowd pleasers was George Mikan, who played for the Minneapolis Lakers. At six feet, ten inches, Mikan was virtually unstoppable under the basket. One of his favorite moves was to catch the ball in the low post, spin toward the basket, and lay the ball up against the backboard for an easy score. He was so effective at doing this that the NBA widened the lane, which was then only six feet wide, to make it harder for him to dominate down under the basket.

With Mikan at center, the Minneapolis Lakers became the NBA's hottest team, winning championships in 1949, 1950, 1952, 1953, and 1954. Because tall, skillful, power players like Mikan were rare at the time, he was as effective on the floor as someone like Shaquille O'Neal is decades later. (And Shaq, of course, is a Laker, too—the Los Angeles version.) In fact, Mikan was such a force in the NBA that when the Lakers went to New York for a game against the Knicks in 1950, the sign outside Madison Square Garden read: TONIGHT, GEORGE MIKAN VERSUS THE KNICKS!

While we have the chance these days to see as many NBA games as we want on television, in the beginning the NBA survived off the income from ticket sales and occasional radio broadcasts of games. Players' salaries were tiny in comparison to the multimillion dollar deals that players make today: a star like Mikan made less than a hundred thousand dollars a year, while the average salary in the NBA today is more than two million dollars a year.

Despite players the caliber of Fulks and Mikan, early NBA games were sometimes downright boring to watch, even for hard-core fans. That was due to stalling, which was a common on-court practice—instead of dribbling and passing, an offensive player would often stand around holding the ball, waiting for a defender to get desperate enough to commit a foul. The result? A trip to the free throw line for the offense. In fact, free throws accounted for many of the points in NBA games—while spectators tried to stay awake!

Stalling led to such boredom fest as the game in 1950 between the Fort Wayne Pistons and the Minneapolis Lakers in which the final score was 19–18. It was (and still is) the lowest-scoring NBA game in history. Imagine sitting through that!

Exasperated by the stalling tactics that so many teams were using, Danny Biasone, owner of the NBA's Syracuse Nationals, came up with a way to speed up the game. He invented the twenty-four-second shot clock. Why twenty-four-seconds? He divided the number of seconds in a 48-minute game (2,880 seconds) by the average number of shots that NBA teams had shot over the previous couple of seasons (120), and got 24. That's how long Biasone thought a team should have to run its plays and take a shot.

The twenty-four-second shot clock was first used in the NBA's 1954–55 season—and it immediately sped up the game. Within the first season of having a shot clock, the number of points that teams scored rose an average of fourteen per game. And the number of teams scoring a hundred points or more in play-off games jumped from three in 1954 to eighteen in 1955! Clearly, the shot clock was the solution to the problem of slow, boring games.

As a result, the NBA never turned back the hands of time. In fact, Biasone's twenty-four-second limit proved so popular that it's still in use today.

With the shot clock came the shooters—guys like Oscar Robertson, Wilt Chamberlain, and Jerry West in the 1960s, Elgin Baylor and Kareem Abdul-Jabbar in the 1970s, Magic Johnson and Larry Bird in the 1980s, and Michael Jordan, Patrick Ewing, and Reggie Miller in the 1990s. As the NBA's hot shooters became stars, so did the NBA.

Key teams have been dominant at various points throughout the NBA's history. Take the Boston Celtics, for example. From the 1956–57 season through the 1968–69 season, the Celtics (with Bill Russell at center and Red Auerbach as coach) were practically unbeatable, racking up eleven NBA championships, including eight in a row. The Celtics returned to glory in the 1980s with Larry Bird on the floor. The Celtics, the New York Knicks, and the Los Angeles Lakers were the powerhouse teams until the 1990s when the Chicago Bulls, led by Michael Jordan, took over as the reigning kings of the NBA.

Between 1990 and 1998 the Bulls won six NBA championships, losing only the 1993–94 and 1994–95 season championships after Jordan quit basketball to play minor-league baseball. But from the time he returned (the 1995–96 season) until the time he retired in January 1999, the Bulls were the undisputed league champs.

Fueled by Jordan's popularity and the resulting surge in the popularity of basketball among people of all ages, the NBA became the hottest professional sports organization around. It was hotter than Major League Baseball or the NFL, hotter than the NHL or PGA, hotter than auto racing or professional tennis. The NBA was (and is) home to some of the most famous, most highly paid athletes in the world.

That seems likely to continue in the twenty-first century. With players like Kobe Bryant, Shaquille O'Neal, Vince Carter, Allen Iverson, and Grant Hill commanding big money for their time on the floor, the NBA remains a source of wealth for great players. While no one player has yet emerged as "the next Michael Jordan" (which sportswriters and shoe companies keep hoping for), the NBA keeps rolling on.

What'd You Say Your Name Was?

Two of the NBA teams of the twenty-first century have been around since the beginning of the league—the Boston Celtics and the New York Knicks.

Others have been around as long, but not in the same place. For example, the Los Angeles Lakers started out as the Minneapolis Lakers—the team moved from Minnesota to California in 1960. Another California team, the Golden State Warriors, began in Philadelphia, making the move west to San Francisco in 1963.

Other teams that have changed location include: the Detroit Pistons (formerly in Fort Wayne, Indiana), the Atlanta Hawks (formerly in St. Louis), and the Washington Bullets (formerly in Baltimore), which have subsequently changed their names to the Bullets.

But while these teams have changed their locations, they've kept their identities—they're still the Pistons, the Hawks, and the Bullets. That's a way of reminding fans of each team's heritage—and of its place in basketball history.

OTHER PRO LEAGUES: THE *ABA*, THE *CBA* AND THE *USBL*

Despite the dominance of the NBA in professional basketball, it has never been the only professional basketball league around. The American Basketball Association (ABA) played an important role from 1967 to 1976 with such legendary players as Julius Erving (Dr. J), George McGinnis, Connie Hawkins, Moses Malone, and David Thompson lighting up the courts in such cities as Philadelphia, Indianapolis, San Antonio, and Denver.

The ABA was a flashy newcomer, playing with a red-white-and-blue ball and allowing three-point outside shots. Its teams played a fast-paced, razzle-dazzle game complete with dramatic slam dunks and plenty of pass-and-shoot plays that kept the ball moving and fans cheering. The ABA changed professional basketball, forcing the rival NBA to speed up its game and recruit more aggressive players with a flair for showmanship. The ABA made professional basketball exciting to watch.

Ironically, it was retired NBA great George Mikan who gave the ABA its best-known symbol: the red-white-and-blue basketball. As a member of the ABA's governing board, Mikan suggested the ball as an attention-getting device for the new league. It worked so well that the ball became an important part of the ABA's advertising and marketing efforts—and it helped make the league a popular addition to America's basketball schedule.

The ABA's players and coaches added to the league's appeal with wardrobes and lifestyles that were hipper and less conventional than those of NBA players and coaches. For instance, Denver Rockets player Lefty Thomas wore a ring on every finger, while Kentucky

Colonels center Artis Gilmore added to his seven-foot, seven-inch height with a five-inch-tall Afro. And Larry Brown, coach of the Carolina Cougars, wore blue jeans to games rather than the traditional dress slacks with sports coat and tie. (Later, Brown, who went on to coach several NBA teams, became one of basketball's best-dressed coaches, sporting tailor-made suits and hand-made shoes.)

But as much as Americans loved the ABA's show, they weren't willing to pay for it. Neither were broadcasters: in the days before cable television, the three major networks (ABC, NBC, and CBS) controlled television, and none was eager to dole out a lot of money for ABA games. While some games were broadcast, most of the television money went to the NBA and to college basketball. Finally, in 1976, the financially struggling ABA closed its doors. When it did, four of its teams joined the NBA: the Indiana Pacers, the San Antonio Spurs, the New Jersey Nets, and the Denver Nuggets.

(Down, but not completely out, the ABA was revived in 2000. As this book goes to the press, it's back on its feet, though its future remains uncertain.)

The Continental Basketball Association (CBA), which lasted from 1946 to 2000, was the NBA's farm-team league. It developed players whom NBA teams sometimes recruited when they had openings on their rosters. The NBA also used the CBA to try out new rules that were under consideration, and to give new referees a chance to develop their officiating skills.

But eventually the CBA became a casualty of the NBA's popularity. During the 1990s, while the NBA was enjoying immense popularity (due largely to the presence of Michael Jordan), the CBA struggled to stay afloat. In 1998 former Detroit Pistons star Isiah Thomas bought the league, promising to get it back in good financial shape. But a year later Thomas was offered the head coaching job with the NBA's Indiana Pacers; when he accepted this position, he was forced to put the CBA up for sale. When no one stepped forward to buy it, the league's team owners, angry at Thomas for what they saw as abandoning them, pulled the plug. The CBA's half century of history ended in a cloud of controversy and complaints.

The United States Basketball League (USBL), which runs a summer league for players who've recently finished college, also serves as a feeder league for the NBA. Many USBL players go on to NBA tryouts—and some even make it on to NBA team rosters.

It's precisely because of a need for new talent that the NBA created a new minor league—the National Basketball Development League (NBDL). Created to help basketball expand both within North America and beyond, the NBDL offers players a chance to sharpen their skills and improve their level of play before ever setting foot on an NBA court. Open to players who are at least twenty years old, the NBDL's eight charter teams were scheduled to kick off their first fifty-six-game season in November 2001.

WOMEN GOT GAME, TOO

Women have been playing professional basketball for years in Europe, Asia, and South America. But in the United States women can trace their involvement in professional leagues back only to 1978, when the Women's

Professional Basketball league was formed. Consisting of eight teams, the league lasted three seasons.

The next major attempt at professional women's basketball came in 1996 with the formation of the eight-team American Basketball League (ABL). That same year, the NBA announced the creation of the Women's National Basketball Association (WNBA), and immediately signed such college and Olympic stars as Rebecca Lobo, Sheryl Swoopes, and Lisa Leslie. The WNBA's first season, 1997–98, was the ABL's last: it couldn't compete with the salaries and visibility that the WNBA could offer to players.

Since then, the WNBA has become a popular addition to the basketball scene. Playing its games during the NBA's summer off season, the WNBA has earned the respect and support of basketball fans around the United States. Its sixteen teams have established a level of play that draws crowds and attracts media coverage, the two things that make the people running any sports league happy.

INTERNATIONAL BASKETBALL

Basketball has been an international sport from the beginning. Among the original eighteen young men in James Naismith's gym class at the Springfield YMCA, four were from Canada and one was from Japan. (You might remember from chapter 1 that Naismith was also a Canadian.)

When they left Springfield and returned to their home countries, those five students took basketball with them. The sport also spread to other countries through the YMCA, which had (and still has) branches throughout the world.

World War I also helped introduce the sport in new places. Many of the American soldiers and sailors stationed in Europe played basketball to stay fit and take their minds off the war. They also taught Europeans how to play the game.

The rapid spread of basketball around the globe meant that even before it became an Olympic sport in 1936, some countries had national teams that competed against each other. By the time that the first International Basketball Conference was held in 1932, eight countries were eager to join together to create the International Basketball Federation.

Within two years membership in the federation had more than doubled, to seventeen countries. And by the 1936 Olympics competition in Berlin there were thirty-two nations in the federation; twenty-three of them sent teams to the competition.

But basketball's international popularity was just getting started. Thanks to satellites that beam basketball broadcasts ranging from college and NBA games to the Olympics, the Pan American Games, and the World Championships around the globe, basketball is popular everywhere from remote villages in Africa to large cities in Asia, Europe, and the Americas.

In 2001 the modern version of the International Basketball Federation had 211 nations spread throughout five regions: Africa, Asia, the Americas, Europe, and Oceania (Australia, New Zealand, and the South Pacific islands).

While the NBA doesn't have teams outside of North America, there are plenty of opportunities for professional players in countries around the world. Teams in Europe regularly recruit players, including Americans.

In fact, for talented players who don't get an NBA offer, playing abroad gives them a chance to be paid well (although not quite as well as the highest-paid NBA players) to play ball.

Not only are good American players going abroad to play professionally, but good foreign players are coming to the United States to play for college and professional teams, too. In fact, NBA teams are more international than ever, with players like Dikembe Mutombo (who's from the Congo), Hakeeem Olajuwon (Nigeria), Toni Kukoc (the former Yugoslavia), and Wang Zhizhi (China) on their rosters.

One of the best-known international players of all time never played in the NBA, however. Oscar Schmidt was a six-foot, eight-inch Brazilian who averaged more than forty-two points a game in the 1988 Olympics, including a record-setting fifty-five points in one game. He went on to play professionally in Italy, becoming the Italian league's leading scorer for eight seasons. When he retired, both of the teams he had played for retired his number.

Besides Italy, which had one of Europe's most powerful professional leagues with fourteen teams, England, France, Spain, Germany, and Greece all have active pro leagues. Outside Europe, there also are professional leagues in places such as Israel, the Philippines, and China. Basketball, the American sport invented by a Canadian, is truly international.

That's No Head Fake—It's a Head!

Some archaeologists claim that basketball was around long before James Naismith nailed up his first

pair of peach baskets. In fact, they say, ancient arti-
facts from centuries earlier suggest that the Mayans,
who once ruled Mexico before the arrival of the
Spanish, actually played a game very similar to
basketball.

But the players on the losing team lost more than
their bragging rights. They lost their heads. Literally.
They were beheaded. Talk about pressure to win!

THE HARLEM GLOBETROTTERS

No look at professional basketball would be complete without the Harlem Globetrotters. Perhaps the best-known basketball team in the world, the Globetrotters have been around since 1927, when a twenty-five-year-old Chicago entrepreneur named Abe Saperstein created them.

The team was originally called Saperstein's New York Globetrotters, even though they weren't from New York and they never left the Midwest region. The entire team consisted of five players and Saperstein, who sometimes took to the court to play if someone else got injured. They all traveled to their games in Saperstein's Model T Ford.

In 1930 Saperstein dropped "New York" from the team's name, replacing it with "Harlem" to emphasize the fact that all of the players (except him) were black. The Harlem Globetrotters they were—and they've remained.

It was during a game in 1939 that the Globetrotters went from being strictly a good basketball team to an entertaining one. They had piled up a 112–5 lead over their opponents when some of the Globetrotter players began clowning around on the court—and the crowd responded with laughter and applause. A new concept was born.

Okay, Saperstein told the team after the game, you can continue to clown around on the floor—as long as you build up a big lead first. Their on-court antics, combined with their talents and skills as basketball players, earned the Globetrotters fame and recognition. By the time of their twentieth anniversary, they had played three thousand games around the United States, and had won more than 90 percent of them!

In 1948 the Globetrotters gained even more attention when they beat the Minneapolis Lakers, the NBA World Championship team with George Mikan at center. It was a close game, with the Globetrotters' Ermer Johnson hitting a twenty-foot, two-handed jump shot at the buzzer for the 61–59 win. The crowd went crazy!

The following year, the two teams met for a rematch at Chicago Stadium. With a crowd of nearly twenty-two thousand fans on hand, the Globetrotters again beat the Lakers, 49–45. This was at a time when the Lakers, with George Mikan at center, were considered the best basketball team in the world—but obviously not every day, since the Globetrotters beat them twice.

The Globetrotters began actually trotting the globe after World War II, first with a seventeen-game series in Hawaii in 1946. Three years later they headed north for a fourteen-game series in Alaska, traveling to one game in a dogsled. By 1951 they were playing games in such places as West Germany, Italy, and Brazil. For the team's twenty-fifth anniversary in 1952, Saperstein booked them on a 108-game tour of the world. It was the first time in basketball history that a team had done such a tour. The Globetrotters have traveled millions of miles since then.

One thing that has made the Globetrotters so popular throughout their long history is the quality of the players. A lot of great players have worn Globetrotter uniforms. One of the team's earliest stars was Reece "Goose" Tatum, who joined the team in 1942. A skillful ball handler—and a natural comedian—Tatum created many of the team's best-known on-the-court comedy routines. Along with Tatum, there was Bernie Price, who scored three-thousand points in the team's 104-game schedule in 1942–43. This was at a time when even the Globetrotters' games were low-scoring affairs, topping out at well under a hundred points per game!

Another Globetrotter, Nathaniel "Sweetwater" Clifton, made basketball history. He was such a gifted player that the New York Knicks recruited him, buying his contract from the Globetrotters for twenty-five thousand dollars. When Clifton made his debut in a Knicks game in 1950, he became the first black player to play in an NBA game.

One of the most famous players ever to wear a Globetrotters uniform was Meadow George Lemon (aka "Meadowlark" Lemon). He played in his first Globetrotters game in 1954, and in his last in 1979. Over the twenty-five years in between, Lemon earned a reputation as a skillful ball handler, sliding across court floors on his knees while dribbling and flipping passes over his shoulder, between his legs, and behind his back. He was also an audience-pleasing comedian, entertaining millions of people around the world with antics such as tossing pails of "water" (actually paper confetti) at folks sitting courtside. Lemon had an infectious enthusiasm that made

people smile—and helped sell lots of tickets to Globetrotters games.

One player whom many people don't realize was once a
Globetrotter was Wilt "The Stilt" Chamberlain. Before
signing on with his first NBA team, the Philadelphia
Warriors, Chamberlain spent the 1958–59 season as a
Globetrotter. Though he was only with the team for a
year, Chamberlain was so respected that when he died in
1999, the Globetrotters wore black patches on their uniforms to honor him—forty years after he'd left for the
NBA.

Throughout the team's long history, the Globetrotters
have recruited great ball players who can be funny in the
process. As a result, they make everything they do look
so simple that it's easy to forget how difficult some of
their ball-handling tricks and antics actually are to do.

While they're an exhibition team, the Globetrotters
have also been basketball innovators. They were the first
to develop the fast break—and the first to run weave patterns when taking the ball down the court. The Globetrotters may be funny to watch, but they're serious about
their basketball skills.

ALL IT TAKES IS A LOT OF HARD WORK

Whether in the NBA, on the Harlem Globetrotters, or
as a member of a local AAU team, what it takes to be a
great player is exactly the same—hard work. Take
Michael Jordan, for instance. Regarded by many basketball fans as the greatest player of all time, Jordan wasn't
just a good showman but also a hard worker. All of the
things that he made look easy on the court, from his

graceful three-point jump shots to his hang-in-the-air jams, were the results of long hours of practice.

When he played for the Chicago Bulls, Jordan was usually the first player at practice and the last to leave. After a home game, he often stayed around and practiced his shooting once the crowd left the arena. Like every other great player, Jordan committed himself to making the extra effort that it took to develop and improve his playing skills.

It's players like this who've taken the game that "Doc" Naismith created and turned it into something special. It's players like you who will continue that tradition. Let's get to work.

Chapter 3

FIT TO PLAY: PHYSICAL FITNESS AND BASKETBALL

Basketball is a very physical sport. Not in the way that football is, of course, with lots of contact and tackles (although NBA games sometimes make basketball seem like a contact sport!). But with all of its running, jumping, passing, and shooting, basketball is a physically demanding sport. It demands that you be physically fit to play it well.

Being fit means you'll be able to keep up with the action on the court. It means you'll have the speed you'll need for fast breaks and for keeping up with players you're guarding. It means you'll have the spring you'll need in your legs for jump shots and rebounds. It means you'll be strong enough to pass, shoot, and defend.

And most important, being fit helps prevent injuries—and helps you recover more quickly if you do get hurt.

BEFORE YOU GET PHYSICAL

If you're going to play basketball in an organized program (at your school or church, a community center, or a YMCA or YWCA), you might be required to get a physical examination first. If you're not, and you haven't had one lately, it's a good idea to get a physical before you go out on the court and get physical.

Ask your parents or guardian to make an appointment for you with your family doctor or pediatrician. Tell the doctor that you're planning on playing basketball, and ask for advice on getting fit and staying healthy both on and off the court.

RUNNING AND JUMPING

Up and down the court, up and down the court, up and down the court. There's no doubt about it—there's a lot of running in a basketball game. That's why you need to run as part of your training. You don't have to run ten miles a day, but you should take time to run laps around the gym (or a school track). If you haven't run much before, take it slowly. If you try to run too far or too fast before your body is ready, you might hurt yourself.

Pace yourself. Run a lap, then walk a lap. Build yourself up gradually, until you're running more laps than you're walking. Just don't expect to get in basketball shape in a day or a week—give your body time to get stronger. If you run regularly, it will.

For variety, try running outdoors, around your neighborhood or in a park. Run in the daytime, and run with a friend (or a few friends). Once again, try running, then walking. When you're running longer distances, never run so hard that you can't carry on a conversation.

Of course, basketball does require short bursts of speed sometimes. That's why you should also do wind sprints—running fast for short distances. One way to do this is to sprint from one side of a basketball court to the other, and back. See how many times you can do this in thirty seconds or a minute. At first you'll probably only be able to do a few, but gradually—as you get stronger— you'll find you can do more.

A good variation of wind sprints is an activity called Death Valley. It's not as bad as it sounds. Starting at one baseline of a full-length basketball court, sprint to the foul line that's nearest to you and back, then to the mid-court line and back, then to the foul line that's farthest from you and back, and finally to the opposite baseline and back. It's a good way to practice not only running fast, but also stopping fast and switching directions—all of which you have to do in a basketball game.

You'll also be doing a lot of jumping, which requires strong legs. Jumping up to grab missed shots (rebounds) and to take shots, jumping up to block shots or to make passes—doing these things means you need to work on strengthening your leg muscles. Running will certainly help you develop them, but so will doing other exercises such as jumping rope and running up and down steps. Or try throwing a basketball against a backboard, then jumping up to catch it. See how many times you can catch it without a miss or a fumble.

WEIGHT TRAINING

College and professional basketball players do weight training to strengthen their arm, chest, and leg muscles. Weight training, however, is something that you should do only with an experienced, trained adult teaching you how to do it correctly and safely.

What can weight training do for you? Obviously, it can

make you stronger. And the stronger your muscles are, the better you'll be at passing, shooting, running, and jumping on the basketball court.

But like any new activity, you have to take it easy when you're working with weights. Don't try to lift too much too soon. In fact, the best thing to do is to use light weights, and gradually increase the number of times that you lift them. Your body will benefit more from lifting three pounds ten times than from lifting ten pounds three times. So don't show off and try to lift heavy weights—you might just end up straining or tearing a muscle, which will keep you out of the weight room and off the basketball court for several weeks or months.

One good way to start getting stronger is to do push-ups. What do push-ups have to do with weight training? Everything. When you do a push-up, what you're doing is pushing the weight of your body up. Instead of pumping iron, you're pumping flesh and bones!

To get started, lie on the floor and put your hands palm down on the floor beneath your shoulders. Now raise yourself up, using your arms for support, and keeping your legs and back straight. Once you're up, lower your body back down. Remember to breathe, slowly and evenly.

Start out doing five at a time, and increase the number as you get stronger. Do three sets of push-ups at a time, if you can. But don't overdo it—it's better for your body to do a few push-ups several times a day than to try to do too many all at once.

Also, don't expect too much too soon. It takes time to get stronger. But if you keep at it, you'll notice a difference after a few weeks. Push-ups strengthen the muscles you use in dribbling (arms and wrists), and in shooting and passing (arms and chest).

The pull-up

Another exercise that uses your body's weight for strength training is pull-ups. All you need is a bar mounted high enough that when you grasp it with both hands, your feet are off the ground. Grab the bar with your hands, palms facing you. Slowly pull your body up until your chin is level with or above the bar. Then lower your body slowly back down. Repeat.

Again, don't overdo it. Give your muscles time to adjust to the new demands you're making of them. Be patient, and you'll see results. Pull-ups develop the muscles in your arms, shoulders, and back, which helps in passing, shooting, and rebounding.

Doing sit-ups

Finally, to develop your groin and lower-back muscles, do sit-ups or crunches. Lie down on the floor with your knees bent and your feet flat on the floor. With your hands behind your neck, slowly raise your shoulders and upper back off the floor, keeping your groin muscles tight. Don't sit all the way up—raise up only a few inches, then lower your body back down slowly. Repeat. Try for sets of five or ten, with a few seconds of rest in between sets.

After all of these exercises, if you're still curious about weight training, talk to an adult (a coach, an athletic trainer, or a phys ed instructor) who can provide you with information about what's right for you. Depending on your age, some types of weight-lifting exercises will be better for developing your muscles (and safer) than others. That's why it's important to learn what to do and how to do it from an adult who knows.

STRETCH OUT

Whether it's a playground game, a team practice, or a tournament final, you should always stretch your muscles before playing basketball. Stretching loosens up your muscles and gets them ready for use, sort of like breaking in a new pair of shoes before wearing them on the court.

Before you stretch, take a five-minute walk around the gym or playground to warm up your muscles. That helps prevent injuries. There are plenty of books and videotapes that teach stretching, but to get you started here are a few basic stretches you can do:

Stretching the hamstring

- **Seated butterfly stretch** While sitting on the floor, put your feet together in front of you. Put your hands on your ankles. Now bend forward slowly, and gently stretch.
- **Hamstring stretch** While sitting on the floor, spread your legs to make a V. Touch your right foot with your left hand, and hold that position for a few seconds. Then do the same thing with your left foot and right hand.
- **Standing quad stretch** While standing, grab your right foot with your right hand. Pull the foot up behind your right leg. Do the same thing with your left foot.
- **Thigh stretch** While standing, spread your legs apart. Bend your right knee as you lean to the right side. Repeat, leaning to the left.
- **Calf stretch** While standing, put your right foot a step ahead of the left. Lean forward on the right leg, bending your knee. Hold this position for a few seconds, then switch legs.
- **Hip stretch** Lie on the floor with your legs straight. Take a deep breath and gradually bring your knees up to your chest. Hold them there for three or four seconds, then lower them while letting your breath out slowly. You can also do this one leg at a time. Try to do sets of five or ten per leg, and the same doing both legs at once.

After you've stretched, it's important to walk or jog again to keep your muscles warm. Also, shoot some baskets. Relax—you're not in a game. Don't try anything fancy. Just get your muscles loosened up. The more ready your body is, the easier it will be to move on the basketball court. And the more fun you'll have playing.

EATING TO PLAY

You want a plate of french fries and a greasy burger, with a tall soft drink on the side. But your mom insists you have a salad and a baked chicken breast, with a glass of milk. She's right.

If you want to play basketball, and play it well, you have to eat your vegetables. And fresh fruits, whole-grain breads and cereals, pasta, rice, fish. In other words, all the good stuff your mom keeps sticking in front of you.

Why? Because what you eat affects how you perform. By eating a variety of good foods (otherwise known as a *balanced diet*), you're giving your body the vitamins and minerals it needs to keep you moving on the court. Food is your body's fuel, so make sure you fuel up with the best food you can.

WATER, WATER, WATER

While the TV commercials tell you to drink soft drinks and sports drinks during and after a basketball game, the truth is that the best thing you can drink is water. After all, your body is made of mostly water—and so is all the sweat that your body produces when you're out there running on the court.

Not only that, but when your body is hot, the best thing to put in it is water. It helps cool you down, and it replaces all of the other water you're losing as you perspire. So forget what the television commercials are telling you. If you really want to help yourself on the court, help yourself to some water. Save the sweet drinks for some other time.

SLEEP TIGHT

There's a great game on ESPN, but it's going to run late. Should you stay up and watch it? Even if your parents don't mind, your body will. Especially if you're going to ask it to get out on the basketball court tomorrow. Instead of having the energy you need to run up and down the court with your teammates, you just might find yourself feeling run down. That's because sleep is an important part of every basketball player's physical fitness program.

Make sure you get plenty of sleep—eight hours or more every night. It's what your body needs to perform at its best, and it's what your mind needs to feel alert. So tape that game and watch it when you have time. You've got to get some shut-eye.

DRESSED TO PLAY

The beauty of playing basketball is that you don't need much equipment or a lot of fancy clothes. The basics—a ball, a good pair of rubber-soled shoes, and a place to play—will do just fine. Of course, there are all kinds of stuff you *can* buy—shoes that cost hundreds of dollars, expensive warm-up jackets and pants, name-brand T-shirts and sweatpants and shorts and jerseys.

But you know what? None of that stuff is going to make you a better ball player, so why bother? Stick with the basics, and you'll be fine. Wear loose-fitting clothes that let you move easily—sweatpants or shorts, a sweatshirt or T-shirt.

Focus on your feet. The most important pieces of

equipment are your shoes and socks. Good ones are like shock absorbers on cars—they'll protect your feet and legs as you run and jump. Your basic shoe choices are high-tops or low-tops. Which one is right for you? High-tops offer more support for your ankles, but some players believe that low-tops allow them to run faster. Whichever type of shoes you choose, make sure they fit well. Shoes that are too tight or too loose will hurt your feet—and slow you down.

As for socks, get thick ones for their cushioning—and to help absorb the sweat from your feet. Thin socks get damp and wrinkle easily, which can lead to blisters—and blisters can stop you from playing ball. If you like thin socks, try wearing two pairs. Experiment a little until you find what works for you.

When it comes to shoes and socks, remember this: your feet are two of the most important body parts in basketball—treat them well. Hobbling down the court because your feet hurt takes all of the fun out of the game.

Once you've taken care of your feet, you can add other things to your wardrobe that feel right for you. Maybe a sweatband to keep the perspiration out of your eyes. Or wristbands to keep your hands dry: sweaty palms can't grip the ball too well. Or a mouth guard to protect your teeth from flying elbows. Or, if you wear eyeglasses, you might want to get a pair of prescription sports glasses with shatterproof safety lenses and an elastic headband to prevent them from slipping down your nose.

But you don't *need* any of those things to play basketball. Forget all of the advertising hype: replica NBA jerseys, warm-up pants with fancy logos on them, and portable, digital scoreboards won't make you a better player. Playing basketball isn't about having a bunch of stuff. It's about having a love for the game.

Fast Facts About Basketball Equipment

- *The first official basketball was made in 1894 by the Overman Wheel Company, which made bicycles in Chicopee Falls, Massachusetts. Before that, soccer balls were used.*
- *The first basketball uniforms were made by the Spalding Company in 1901. Three types of pants were available: knee-length, padded pants; short, padded pants; and knee-length tights. Shirts were either sleeveless or had three-quarter-length sleeves (like football jerseys).*
- *The first basketball shoes were made in 1903, again by Spalding. They had "suction soles" that were guaranteed not to slip.*

MOTIVATION: IT'S ALL IN YOUR HEAD

The dream of many young basketball players is to make it professionally, to play in the NBA or the WNBA. That's a wonderful dream, but it shouldn't be your only motivation for playing the sport.

In his 1941 book, *Basketball: Its Origin and Development,* James Naismith outlined some of the benfits of playing basketball. He said that basketball helps players develop the following things:

- Initiative, which is your ability to figure out what to do in new situations.

- Agility, which is the ability of your body to move easily and quickly.
- Accuracy, which is your ability to successfully do what you attempt to do.
- Alertness, which is your ability to respond instantly to whatever's happening around you.
- Cooperation, which is your ability to to work with other people to achieve a common goal.
- Skill, which is your ability to do correctly what you need to do, when you need to do it.
- Reflex, which is the ability of your body to do what you need to do without your mind having to think about doing it.
- Speed, which is your ability to move from one place to another rapidly.
- Self-confidence, which is your ability to do things without doubting yourself.
- Self-sacrifice, which is your ability to consider someone else's needs (such as those of your teammates) more important than your own.
- Self-control, which is your ability to keep your emotions and behavior in check so they don't interfere with what you're doing.
- Sportsmanship, which is your ability to win or lose gracefully, and to recognize and appreciate others' accomplishments in the process.

So there are a lot of benefits to playing basketball beyond an NBA contract. Which is a good thing, considering how few players ever actually make it to that level.

Consider the numbers. More than one million high school students play basketball in the United States every year. How many players are in the NBA in any year? Less than 350. In the WNBA? Less than 150. Do the math: the odds are against any young player becoming a professional.

But of course, a few do. That's what keeps dreams alive. And dreaming of a professional basketball career can be a lot of fun, but it shouldn't be the reason you play basketball. Be motivated by a desire to improve your skills, to get stronger, to learn more about the game, to be part of a team. Motivate yourself to become the best that you can be as a player, a student, a person. Then, if your dream of playing professionally comes true, it will be something extra on top of all of your other accomplishments.

Remember this: the beauty of the sport of basketball is that it doesn't require much equipment. You don't *need* anything fancy to get up a game. Just a ball, a court, and a few friends. Keep it simple. Keep it fun. That's the best motivation of all.

Basketball Safety

Compared to more violent sports such as football and hockey, basketball is pretty safe. But that doesn't mean it's injury-free or danger-free. Here are a few tips on staying safe on the court.

First, whether you're playing indoors or outdoors, check the condition of the basket and backboard. Is the basket securely attached to the backboard? Is the backboard securely attached to the pole or braces supporting it? If the answer to either of those questions is no, walk away. You don't need a loose basket or backboard falling down on your head.

Speaking of backboard supports, is the pole supporting the backboard padded? If not, be careful.

Running into an unpadded pole while chasing a loose ball is no fun.

Watch out for those nets made from metal chains! Not only do they lack the sweet "swish" sound you get from dropping a shot through a nylon net, but they also hurt if you take a swipe at a shot in the air and smack your hand or wrist into the chain instead.

Avoid unlit courts at night. Basketball in the dark isn't nearly as much fun as it sounds if you get a ball in the face or trip over something you didn't see on the court. Also, if it's a public court, you never know who's going to be lurking around there after dark.

Pass on games against bullies—you know, the players who use basketball as an excuse to shove people around, intimidate them, even hurt them. It's just a game. It's not worth risking your life to play it.

Oh, and finally, tie those shoes! There's nothing that looks worse (or feels worse) than tripping over a loose shoestring when you're driving in for a layup— and landing facefirst on the court.

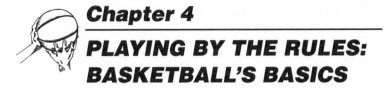

Chapter 4

PLAYING BY THE RULES: BASKETBALL'S BASICS

Every game has its rules, and basketball is no exception. And like other sports, basketball's rules have grown more complex over the years. Today there are special rules for different levels of the sport—there are high school rules, for example, as well as college, professional, and international rules.

For instance, high school games consist of four eight-minute quarters or two sixteen-minute halves, while college, international, and WNBA games consist of two twenty-minute halves. NBA games are four twelve-minutes quarters. Also, in most states there is no shot clock (which limits the time the team with the ball has to take a shot) for high school games, while college men's teams have a thirty-five-second shot clock, women's college and WNBA teams have thirty-second clocks, and the NBA has a twenty-four-second clock.

While there are other such differences from one level of the sport to another, the basic rules of the sport—the ones that control what players can and cannot do on the court—are the same. And have remained so for a long time. Some of the basic rules, in fact, go back to James Naismith's original list of thirteen.

As you recall from chapter 1, Naismith's rules included ones prohibiting a player from running with the ball and intentionally hitting or tripping another player. Doing either of those things resulted in a foul, just as it does today.

However, Naismith also ruled that three fouls in row by one team would give the other team a point; today there are no free points for fouls, but the player who has been fouled gets one or two free throws (depending on whether or not the foul took place when the player was taking a shot). Over the course of the game, a good free-throw-shooting team can put several extra points on the scoreboard.

Naismith's rules also stated that:

- A team scored a goal when one of its players threw the ball into the basket. (Still true.)
- A player throwing a ball inbounds had five seconds to do so, or the other team got the ball. (Once again, still true.)
- The referee was responsible for keeping track of a game's score, as well as keeping track of the time left in the game. (Today, the referee gets help with these tasks from the scorekeeper and the time-keeper.)
- The team that made the most goals won the game. (Nothing has changed here.)

While some of Naismith's rules are familiar today, others have been altered or discarded over the years. And a lot of new ones have been added, which is why sometimes you might find yourself wondering what's going on when you watch a game. Basketball, which began as a sport with a few simple rules, has gotten more complex over time.

But we're going to keep it simple, and focus on basketball's basic rules. We'll leave the complicated stuff to the experts—the officials and statisticians who keep track of it all.

James Naismith's Original Thirteen Rules of Basketball

The ball to be an ordinary Association [sic] football. *

1. *The ball may be thrown in any direction with one or both hands.*
2. *The ball may be batted in any direction with one or both hands (never with the fist).*
3. *A player cannot run with the ball. The player must throw it from the spot on which he catches it; allowance to be made for a man who catches the ball when running at a good speed.*
4. *The ball must be held in or between the hands; the arms or body must not be used for holding it.*
5. *No shouldering, holding, pushing, tripping, or striking, in any way the person of an opponent shall be allowed; the first infringement of this rule by any person shall count as a foul, the second shall disqualify him until the next goal is made, or, if there was evident intent to injure the person, for the whole of the game, no substitute allowed.*
6. *A foul is striking at the ball with the fist, violation of Rules 3, 4, and as described in Rule 5.*
7. *If either side makes three consecutive fouls, it shall count as a goal for the opponents. (Consecutive means without the opponents in the meantime making a foul.)*

---

* In this instance, what Naismith calls a "football" is what we know as a soccer ball.

8. *A goal shall be made when the ball is thrown or batted from the grounds into the basket and stays there, providing those defending the goal do not touch or disturb the goal. If the ball rests on the edge and the opponent moves the basket, it shall count as a goal.*

9. *When the ball goes out of bounds, it shall be thrown into the field and played by the person first touching it. In case of a dispute, the umpire shall throw it straight into the field. The throw-in is allowed five seconds. If he holds it longer it shall go to the opponent. If any side persists in delaying the game, the umpire shall call a foul on them.*

10. *The umpire shall be judge of the men and shall note fouls and notify the referee when three consecutive fouls have been made. He shall have the power to disqualify men according to Rule 5.*

11. *The referee shall be judge of the ball and shall decide when the ball is in play, in bounds, to which side it belongs, and shall keep the time. He shall decide when a goal has been made, and keep account of the goals, with any other duties that are usually performed by a referee.*

12. *The time shall be two fifteen minute halves, with five minutes rest in between.*

13. *The side making the most goals in that time shall be declared the winners. In case of a draw, the game may, by agreement of the captains, be continued until another a goal is made.*

THE COURT

In the beginning, basketball courts were shorter and narrower than they are today. As you discovered earlier, the first courts were only fifty feet long and thirty-five feet wide. That's small compared to today's high school, college, and professional courts, which are ninety-four feet long and fifty feet wide. If you tried playing on one of the courts from the past, it'd probably feel like you were playing in a classroom rather than in a gym.

The markings on the floor aren't for decoration—they serve specific purposes. The most important ones are:

- **The midcourt line** A basketball court is divided into two halves that are exactly alike. The midcourt line separates them. During a game, the half where the offensive team's basket is located is called the *forecourt*. The half where the defensive team's basket is located is called the *backcourt*. That means that one team's forecourt is always the other team's backcourt. The midcourt line is also known as the *timeline,* because the team with the ball has ten seconds to get the ball from the backcourt into the forecourt, or it loses possession.
- **The sidelines** These are the lines that mark the two sides of the court and separate in-bounds territory from out-of-bounds territory.
- **The baselines** These are the lines that mark the two ends of the court and (like the sidelines) separate in-bounds territory from out-of-bounds territory.
- **The center circle** This is the circle in the middle of the midcourt line. This is where the game-opening

tip-off (when a referee tosses the ball into the air and a player from each team jumps into the air and tries to tip it to a teammate) takes place.

- **The free throw (or foul) lane**   This is the rectangle at each end of the court; there's a circle at the end of the lane facing the midcourt line. It's also known as the *key* (because of its shape) or the *paint* (because it's painted a different color than the rest of the lines on the court). When a player is taking a *free throw* (the unguarded shot that a player gets to take when a referee decides another player has committed a foul—it's also known as a *foul shot*), the players from both teams line up along the sides of the lane.
- **The free throw (or foul) line**   This is the line at the end of the free throw lane farthest from the basket—fifteen feet away, to be exact. This is the line that a player shooting a free throw must stand behind.
- **The free throw (or foul) circle**   This is the circle (half solid line, half broken line) at the end of the foul lane. It marks the area that no player can enter when another player is shooting a free throw.
- **The three-point arc**   This is the large semicircle at each end of the court. Any goal made by a player standing outside the arc is worth three points.

THE BASKET, THE BACKBOARD, AND THE BALL

While Naismith used peach baskets for his goals, most people today use something else—like wastebaskets and laundry baskets! Just kidding. Today's baskets are stronger and more specialized. And when you make a basket, you don't have to climb a ladder to get the ball back out!

Basket rims these days are made of strong metal to hold up to the battering and banging they take from hard jams and slams. Breakaway rims are mounted on tightly wound springs that allow them to fold down when players grab them or balls slam down on them too hard; then the rims swing back into place. A regulation rim is ten feet off the ground and eighteen inches around, making it a bull's-eye for hot shooters and the broad side of a barn for those who can't hit it.

The net hanging from a rim today typically is made of nylon cord, which holds up well both indoors and out. However, some courts in public parks and on school playgrounds have steel chain-link nets, which are practically indestructible under even the heaviest of use.

While backboards come in different shapes (rectangular, square, arched) and sizes, a regulation backboard is six feet wide by three and a half feet tall. It's made of Plexiglas—though other types of backboards may be made of wood or metal. Among players, backboards are known as the *glass* (for Plexiglas) or the *boards* (both backboards in a full-court game).

Then there is the ball. A regulation basketball is nine inches in diameter, and it's made of either rubber or leather. Rubber balls are best for outdoor use because they're rugged enough to stand up to hot and cold temperatures, and to landing in water puddles and mud. They can also stand up to bouncing on asphalt, rocks, concrete, and clay.

Leather balls aren't quite as tough. While they're smooth and wonderful to handle on indoor courts, they don't do well outdoors. Leave a leather ball out in the rain, or dribble it on rough surfaces, and it'll be ruined in no time. Though they're more fragile, leather balls have a sense of history that rubber balls lack: after all, leather was the only type of material that basketballs were made from for many years. That may be why they're still popular and used by high school, college, and professional teams around the world.

THE PLAYERS AND THEIR POSITIONS

The total number of players on a basketball team varies from one level to another: an NBA team can have twelve, for example, while a high school team may have more than that (or fewer). But no matter what level of organized basketball you're playing—from an elementary school league to the NBA—each team in a game can only have five players on the court at a time.

Why only five? In the early years of the sport, there was no limit on the number of players who could be on the floor at the same time. In one game at Cornell University, there were a hundred players in a single game—fifty on each side! Finally, in 1897, Naismith and others involved with the new sport agreed that there had to be a set number of players allowed on the court during a game, and that number was set at five.

As a result of that limit, the players on the court were divided into five positions: two guards, two forwards, and a center for each team. The guards are responsible for bringing the ball upcourt, setting up plays (a *play* is a pattern of passes and moves made by the offensive team's players), and taking shots from outside of the free throw lane or behind the three-point arc. The forwards are responsible for taking shots in or just outside of the free throw lane, and for pulling down rebounds. The tallest person on the team, the center is an inside shot maker, either taking or setting up teammates to take layups (driving in close to the basket and banking the ball off the backboard), hook shots (tossing the ball overhead in a hooklike motion), and slam dunks (jumping into the air and jamming the ball into the basket with a lot of force). The center also handles much of the rebounding.

Over time, specialized versions of those positions have been developed. Today, there are *small forwards,* who do a lot of inside shooting; *point guards,* who signal the plays and take outside shots; *power forwards,* who rebound and take inside shots; and *shooting guards,* who do just what the name says—they shoot, a lot. But the center is still the center—and often, the center of the action.

All teams have players on the bench as well as on the court during a game. This is so that when someone on the court is injured, tired, or in foul trouble, one of the bench players can be sent in as a substitute while the other player leaves the court for a rest. Some bench players also have specific skills—a great outside shot, for example, or strong defensive abilities—which cause their coaches to put them on the court at certain points in a game.

A coach might put a substitute into a game because another player on the court needs to rest for a few minutes, or because the team is having trouble and needs another rebounder, shot blocker, or three-point shooter on the floor. Substitutions can occur whenever the game has stopped (during a time-out, after a foul has been called, at the end of a quarter or half). Before going onto the floor, the substitute player must check in at the scorer's table, which is on the sideline, by the midcourt line.

OFFENSIVE AND DEFENSIVE TEAMS

In any game, there are two teams on the court at the same time. The team that has the ball in its possession is called the offensive team: its players are trying to get the ball past the other team's players to make a basket. The defensive team is the team that's trying to prevent the offensive team from making a basket. Of course, every time one team gets the ball, it becomes the offensive team, and every time it loses the ball, it becomes the defensive team. So the teams are constantly changing roles, which means their players have to be able to play both offense and defense.

In an official game, there is also the *home team* and the *visitors* (or *away*) *team*. The home team is the team whose court is being used for the game; the visitors are the team who've come to play there. The home team usually wears light-colored uniforms, while the visitors wear dark uniforms.

SCORING

For the first few years after basketball was invented, each basket that a team scored was worth one point. In 1897 that was changed to two points for each basket made, and one point for each free throw made. The only change in scoring since then came with the introduction of the three-point shot in the 1980s. Today there are three ways to score points: one point for each free throw that goes in the basket, two points for each basket made from inside the three-point arc, and three points for each shot made from outside the arc.

TICK-TOCK, TICK-TOCK: THE CLOCKS

Time is an important part of any basketball game. That's why, in addition to the usual clock that provides the correct time, there are other types of clocks on gymnasium and arena scoreboards.

A basketball game is divided into quarters or halves. Most high school games have four eight-minute-long quarters. NBA games have four twelve-minute-long quarters. College, international, and WNBA games have two twenty-minute halves. Whether measured in quarters or halves, an official *game clock* keeps track of the minutes, seconds, and tenths of a second remaining in each quarter or half. (It also times the ten- or fifteen-minute halftime breaks.)

The other important clock in college and professional basketball is the *shot clock*. In NBA games the offensive team has twenty-four seconds to take a shot or lose possession of the ball. For men's college basketball, it's thirty-five seconds; for women's college and professional teams, it's thirty seconds. The shot clock keeps track of those seconds: if the clock hits zero and the offensive team hasn't taken a shot, a buzzer or horn goes off, letting referees know that time is up. The team that failed to take a shot has to give the ball to its opponents.

These two clocks are more important to players during a game than the clock providing the actual time of day. Knowing how much time is left in a quarter or half, or how much time your team has to take a shot affects what you decide to do on the court: knowing that it's 9 P.M. doesn't.

REFEREES AND OTHER OFFICIALS

A regulation basketball game has three types of officials: the referees, the scorekeeper, and the timekeeper. The referees (those men or women running up and down the court with whistles in their mouths) are responsible for keeping order on the court. They make sure that everyone plays by the rules, and they decide what the penalties are for those players who violate the rules— anything from losing possession of the ball for stepping out of bounds while holding the ball to being charged with a foul for slapping another player's arm (accidentally or not) during a shot.

(Yes, even accidental contact with the player who has the ball can result in a referee calling a foul on you. In fact, a good offensive player will try to make you commit a foul by faking a move in one direction so you begin to move, then reversing direction so you end up making contact.)

Like players, referees have to keep themselves in good physical condition, because they run up and down the court all throughout a game—with no substitutions. They also have to keep their cool when being yelled at by players or coaches or fans who disagree with their decisions. Being a referee is a hard job, but they're the ones who help keep the game civilized.

Do referees make mistakes? Of course—they're only human. But most of the time, even if an official realizes he or she has made a bad call, the game simply goes on. Only if the game is really close or time is really tight, or if another official strongly disagrees with a call, will a questionable decision be reviewed. At that point, game officials will look at a replay of the game video (nearly all games from the high school level on up are videotaped these days) to determine whether or not the right call was made. If the decision is that the call was right, it stands; if the decision is that it was wrong, then it is corrected.

No less important, and no less difficult, is being the official scorekeeper for a game. The scorer is responsible not only for keeping track of the correct score of the game, but also for keeping track of how many points, rebounds, and fouls each player in the game has.

Finally, there's the official timekeeper who (you guessed it) keeps track of time left in the game. That's not always as easy as it sounds, because the timekeeper has to be alert to both the time showing on the game clock and the time showing on the shot clock (if the game has one). Both clocks have to be stopped whenever a referee stops the game, and restarted at the same time that the referee blows the whistle to restart the game. That's why there are often two timekeepers for a game with both a game clock and a shot clock.

CALLING THE SHOTS: THE COACH

If you're playing basketball in an organized league, your team has a coach. Whether your coach is a paid professional or someone's mom or dad, the responsibilities are the same. *A coach is in charge of the team.*

That means that your coach is the person who decides what's going to happen during games and practice. He or she decides who is going to play which position, what type of defense the team is going to play, which offensive plays to run and when to run them, and how long each player is going to remain on the court (or on the bench).

It's a coach's duty to help you become a better player, and to help the team become a better team. You might not always like the decisions that your coach makes, or you might not always agree with what he or she says, but if you're going to play on a basketball team, you have to listen to your coach. And you have to play the game the way your coach wants it played.

A good coach is a teacher. If you pay attention, you'll learn something—maybe a little, maybe a lot. But as a player, you should always be willing to try things out, even if they don't make sense to you at the time. Remember, a coach has to think about the entire team, about doing things for the benefit of the team, not for the benefit of individual players.

You might not know why your coach makes a decision, but you have to respect his or her right to make it. And you have to accept your coach's decisions without complaining about them. Constantly questioning or ignoring your coach guarantees you'll spend a lot of time sitting on the bench—or in the stands after you're kicked off the team.

In the end, the coach is the one who calls the shots.

TIME-OUTS AREN'T JUST FOR STOPPING THE CLOCK

A time-out does just what it says: it takes time out of the game—and it stops both the game clock and the shot clock. That's especially important during games which are close right up to the end.

Time-outs are also an important part of basketball strategy. A time-out may be called by a coach who wants to talk to his or her players, or by a player or the coach of the team that has possession of the ball. A referee can also call a time-out, but for now we're only talking about a coach's or player's time-out.

A coach calls a time-out—or signals to a player to call one—to talk about what's happening (or needs to happen) on the court. For example, if a team has the ball, a coach might call a time-out to set up a play. If a team is on defense, a coach might call a time-out to change the type of defense the team is playing.

One of the most famous time-outs in basketball history came in the 1976 NBA Finals. A game between the Phoenix Suns and the Boston Celtics had gone into two overtimes, and with one second left, John Havlicek scored for the Celtics, putting Boston up 111–110.

The Suns coach Paul Westphal (a former Celtics player) called a time-out, even though he knew that his team had already taken all of the time-outs it was allowed. The result was a technical foul—one free throw for the Celtics, which Jo Jo White made.

But at that time, NBA rules stated that after a technical foul, the other team got the ball back. So the Suns inbounded from half court, and Garfield Heard took a twenty-five-footer, making it at the buzzer. This was in the era before the three-pointer, so once again the game was tied—and went into triple overtime. But in the end the Suns lost.

More important, however, as a result of Westphal's trick, the NBA's technical foul rule was changed. A similar violation today would result in two shots and possession of the ball by the shooting team. While coaches today can no longer do what Westphal did, they still can use time-outs to talk about or change their teams' strategies.

BREAKING THE RULES: FOULS AND OTHER NO-NOS ON THE COURT

There are three types of fouls: personal, offensive, and technical. None of them is good, though sometimes fouls are unavoidable.

A *personal foul* is something that one player does to another (most often, a defensive team's player to the offensive player with the ball), such as shoving or tripping or colliding, either accidentally or on purpose. It results in one or more free throws if the player who was fouled was taking a shot; if not, it results in the fouled player's team getting to throw the ball in from out of bounds. In high school and college, each player is allowed a total of five personal fouls before *fouling out* (having to sit out the rest of the game). In professional basketball, players are allowed six personal fouls.

An *offensive foul* is one committed by a player whose team has the ball. For example, if a player who has the ball runs into a player from the other team after that player has stopped moving, it's a *charging foul*. The penalty for charging and other offensive fouls is the loss of the ball to the other team.

A *technical foul* is something that a player or coach does that a referee considers poor sportsmanship—arguing with a referee's decision, throwing an object on the floor, or generally acting badly. It results in a free throw (and possession of the ball) for the opposing team. After two technical fouls, a player or coach is ejected from the game and must leave the floor.

In the NBA there's a fourth type of foul known as a *flagrant foul*. It's called when an official thinks that one player has fouled another not only intentionally, but unnecessarily or too forcefully. This happens, for instance, in games where players get frustrated or angry, tempers flare, and one player knocks another player down with a hard shove under the basket. Too many flagrant fouls during a season can get a player suspended and fined.

When is a foul, a foul, and when is it not? That's up to a referee to decide, but here's a quick rule of thumb: if you do something to another player that you know you aren't supposed to do (and it involves physical contact or it injures that player), then you've committed a foul. And you (and your team) will be punished according to the rules.

There Are Fouls That Are Offensive, Then There Are Offensive Fouls

It's not just defensive players who commit fouls; offensive players also commit them, although not as often. (Or maybe it's just that they don't get caught as often.) The three most common types of offensive fouls are:

- **Charging** *This happens when an offensive player with the ball runs into a defensive player who is standing still.*
- **Moving pick** *This happens when an offensive player who has set a pick on a defensive player tries to continue to block that player by moving when the defender moves.*
- **Over the back** *This occurs when an offensive player tries to grab a rebound by reaching over the back of a defensive player, bumping or shoving the defender in the process.*

An offensive foul is included in the running total of personal fouls that a player commits during the game—which means a couple of offensive fouls does just as much to get a player in foul trouble as a couple of defensive fouls.

In addition to fouls, there are some other important rule violations you need to know about—a *lane violation*, for example. That's when any player on either team steps into the free throw lane while a player is shooting a foul shot. This might happen, for instance, if a player gets too eager to get in position for the rebound in case the shot doesn't go in. If a player from the defensive team does it, the player taking the shot gets an extra attempt if the first one misses. If an offensive player does it and the shooter makes the foul shot, the shot doesn't count.

Then there's *traveling*. Do it on vacation, not on the basketball court. Traveling is when a player who has the ball moves without dribbling the ball—that's never a good move. The penalty is loss of possession. If you have the ball and you're moving your feet, remember to dribble, too.

The vertical version of traveling is called *up-and-down*. That's when the player with the ball jumps without either shooting or passing. Let's say you jump up, intending to pass the ball to a teammate, but you realize once you're in the air that it's a risky pass—that's too bad. If you leave the ground with the ball, you have to come down without it, or you've committed an up-and-down violation.

But you can have both feet on the floor and still have problems. Take dribbling, for instance, or rather *double dribbling*. Double dribbling occurs when a player stops dribbling the ball, holds it, then starts dribbling again. Or when a player touches the ball with both hands while dribbling. Either way, the other team gets the ball.

Another thing that makes referees blow their whistles is the *three-second violation*. That's when a player on the offensive team moves into the free throw lane hoping to receive a pass and take a shot, or to get in position for a rebound, but stays in the lane for more than three seconds. Offensive team players can step in and out of the lane as often as they want—they just can't stay there longer than three seconds at a time. If they do, they'll hear the shriek of a silver whistle—and the other team will have the ball.

Sometimes a referee will call for a *ten-second violation*. When one team has scored a goal, the other team has ten seconds after passing the ball inbounds to get it back across the midcourt line. Failing to do this gives the other team possession of the ball.

Also, there's a violation commonly known as *over-and-*

back, which happens when the offensive team gets the ball across the midcourt line before the ten seconds are up, but then passes it back to a player standing on the other side of that line. Not a smart move—the result is loss of the ball. Remember, once the ball has crossed the midcourt line, it can't go back—unless your opponents have it. (And if it does, they will.)

Another common violation is *goaltending.* That's when a defensive player knocks the ball away from the basket when it's on the way down toward the basket, or touches the rim or net when the ball has been shot. While you can block a shot when the ball is on its way up into the air, you can't interfere with its trip down toward the basket. The penalty for goaltending? The offensive team gets the points for making the basket—even if the shot itself might have missed.

And a word about *kicking:* save it for soccer. If a defensive player kicks the ball during a game, the other team gets to keep possession of the ball. If an offensive player kicks the ball and it ends up out of bounds, the other team gets possession.

As for *out of bounds*—it probably seems obvious, but it's still important to keep in mind. Anytime the ball touches the sidelines or baselines, or the floor beyond them, it's considered out of bounds. The team that touched the ball last as it was going out of bounds is considered the one that caused it to go out, and the other team gets possession.

Anytime the offensive team does something that causes it to lose possession of the ball, they've committed what's called a *turnover.* If you're a pastry lover, you probably know all about one kind of turnover—the apple or cherry kind. It's sweet. But a turnover on the basketball court is not.

The best thing you can do as a player is to know the basic rules about what you can and cannot do on the court, and then stick to them. Cheaters may win games now and then, but they never have the satisfaction of knowing that they've won because they played by the rules. When you play by the rules, you've won even if the scoreboard says you've lost.

Chapter 5

SMOOTH MOVES TAKE PRACTICE: LEARNING TO HANDLE THE BALL

When you watch professional basketball players like Vince Carter and Kobe Bryant, it's easy to get the idea that basketball is all about fancy moves. But it's not. Basketball is about mastering some basic ball-handling skills—dribbling, passing, receiving, rebounding. If you learn to do these things well, you'll be well on your way to success on the court. Then you can work on a fancy move or two.

But until then, stick to the basics and you can't go wrong. Even Vince and Kobe had to start somewhere.

HOLDING THE BALL

How do you hold a basketball? With your hands. But did you know there's a right way and a wrong way to hold the ball?

First, the wrong way. Never hold a ball with your hands on opposite sides. Why? Because that makes it hard to control. Whether you're passing or shooting, the farther apart your hands are on the ball, the more difficult it is to control what happens when you release it.

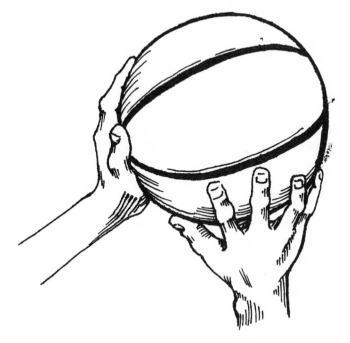

Correct positioning of the hands

So what's the right way to hold the ball? With your hands. Just kidding! The right way to hold a basketball is with one hand slightly higher on the ball than the other. Your hands should be close enough together that you can form a T with your thumbs, with the upper hand forming the crossbar of the T, and your lower hand forming the vertical bar.

To practice holding the ball correctly, try this. Standing comfortably, with your feet spread apart no farther than your shoulders, hold the ball with your thumbs in the T position. Then flip the ball out in front of you, putting a spin on it by snapping your wrists forward as you release the ball. It should hit the floor about three feet in front of you and bounce back to you. When you catch it, try to have your hands positioned so they'll naturally grip the ball in the T position once again.

Doesn't sound too exciting, does it? It isn't. But it is a good way to practice catching and holding the ball properly. And being able to do this without thinking about it can be very important in an actual basketball game. Ball control can make the difference in a close game—and lack of control can lead to turnovers, steals, and bobbled passes.

DRIBBLING

In basketball's early years, players never bounced (or *dribbled*) the ball. To prevent a steal, they passed the ball or rolled it on the floor in front of them. Rolling gradually gave way to bouncing the ball in place, which then turned into dribbling on the move. An early form of dribbling was called overhead dribbling. A player would run down the court while batting the ball in the air! Today, of course, you can't do that, but you can dribble the ball while walking or running.

That's why one of the most important ball-handling skills you can develop is the dribble. The better you are at dribbling, the more control you'll have of the ball and yourself. If you're a good dribbler, you can get the ball to the right place on the court to set up shots for yourself and your teammates. You can also move the ball quickly up the court during fast breaks, and force defensive players to foul you when they try to steal the ball. Being able to dribble well is an important part of being an all-around player.

Learning to dribble well requires practice. First of all, never slap the ball with the palm of your hand. Use your fingertips to control its bounce. Don't stiffen your wrist—keep it loose. Hold your hand flat while you're dribbling, and keep it centered over the ball. Also, work on dribbling with a steady rhythm (like keeping the beat in music), and making the ball bounce low enough that it's hard to steal.

After all, one thing that every defender wants to do is steal the ball from you, and one way to do that is to slap it away if you get careless and don't protect that ball while you're dribbling it. That's why you hunch a little to protect the ball from the other team's players. Also, don't look at the ball! Why? Because, if you're watching the ball, you can't see your teammates—or any opposing player who might be closing in on you.

Learn to dribble well with each hand. That's important because you need to be able to dribble the ball with the hand that's farther from the player who's guarding you. Keep the dribble to the outside, by your knee. Doing so puts your body between the defender and the ball, making it more difficult to slap the ball away or steal it.

Learning to dribble with either hand takes practice. Start by dribbling the ball while standing still. Dribble it twenty-five times with one hand, then twenty-five times with the other. Switch back and forth until you can complete all twenty-five dribbles with each hand without losing control of the ball.

Now practice dribbling on the move. While walking the length of the basketball court (or your driveway, or a park sidewalk), dribble with one hand, then return while dribbling with the other hand. Keep practicing until you can do this exercise without losing control of the ball. Then do it while running slowly. Increase your speed as you get more confident in your dribbling. Eventually you should be able to run pretty fast and still dribble the ball.

Once you can dribble well with each hand, it's time to practice your *crossover*. That's moving the ball from one hand to the other while dribbling. This will let you move in any direction while still controlling the ball and keeping it away from the player guarding you.

To work on crossing over, try dribbling with one hand while taking two steps, then switch to the other hand and take two steps. Keep switching back and forth as you two-step the width of a gym floor. Once you feel confident in your crossover skills, do this same exercise the length of the gym and back.

Also, work on dribbling as you run, then as you stop quickly, then as you start running again. That's a move called *stop and go*. You should be able to dribble while moving at a variety of speeds—and while changing the direction that you're moving. Practice dribbling while walking and running backward. Set up a few chairs in a line, and practice dribbling while weaving around the chairs.

You don't need to be able to dribble between your legs or behind your back to be a good ball handler. You just need to be able to control the ball when you're dribbling it. That's an accomplishment you can be proud of!

PASSING

Another ball-handling skill that's as important as dribbling is passing. In fact, passing is the fastest way to get a ball up the court and in scoring position. It's also the heart of teamwork: a team with players who pass the ball to each other is a better team than one that allows one or two players to have the ball most of the time.

Passing is based on a three-part process: *step, snap,* and *follow through.* The first thing you do as you pass the ball is take a *step* forward (without moving your pivot foot). Then you *snap* your wrists as you release the ball. And finally you *follow through* by extending your arms as if you're reaching for something on the other side of the court. Teach yourself to *step, snap,* and *follow through,* and you'll be on your way to being a good team player.

There are three basic passes—the chest pass, the bounce pass, and the overhead pass. There are others, as well, such as the *baseball pass* (a court-length pass thrown like a baseball), the *lob pass* (a high pass that arches over the heads of defenders), and the *behind-the-back pass* (a one-handed, waist-level pass flipped around a player's back). But let's stick to the three basic passes: they're the ones you'll use the most.

With the *chest pass,* you use both hands to snap the ball to a teammate. Release the ball at chest level. The player you're passing to should be able to catch the ball also at chest level. Throw it hard enough to get it to your teammate, but not so hard that he or she can't control it.

For a *bounce pass,* you also use both hands, but instead of releasing the ball at chest level, you pick a spot on the floor about halfway (or two-thirds of the way) between you and a teammate. Take your step, and snap the

Chest pass

Bounce pass

ball so it bounces on that spot. Bounce it hard enough that it makes it to your teammate.

Finally, the *overhead pass* is a good one to use when you want to throw the ball farther than you can with a chest pass or a bounce pass. Again using both hands, lift the ball over your head, step, and snap it hard enough to cover the distance between you and a teammate.

As with any other skill, passing takes practice, something you should do as often as you can. If there's no one around to help you practice, use a gym wall, the side of a building, or some other solid surface as your target. Do each of the three passes as many times as you can. Work on *step, snap,* and *follow through* until you can do each without thinking.

Also, work on controlling your passes as much as you can. Practice passing from different distances, so you'll learn how to pass at the right speed. A pass that's thrown too softly or too hard can cause a turnover.

Part of controlling your passes is learning to "read" what's happening on the court. If there are several defensive players in an area around the player you want to pass the ball to, don't make the pass. Why? Because there's a possibility that it will be intercepted.

Also, don't make the same type of pass every time and don't be too obvious about when you're going to make a pass. Why? Because defensive players will know what you're going to do and they'll try to steal the ball.

Never make a pass to someone who isn't paying attention. Before you pass, make eye contact so your teammate knows the ball is coming. That way the ball won't get stolen or bobbled out of bounds.

Something else to avoid—fancy passes. Forget about the between-the-legs and no-look passes you see in NBA

Overhead pass

games. Those are done by players with many years of experience—players who know how to make those types of passes as naturally as you should know how to *step, snap,* and *follow through*. It's more important to do basic passes well than to risk losing the ball because you're trying to show off by doing something fancy.

Work on controlling both the ball and yourself. Don't pass just to get rid of the ball. A good pass is one that helps move the ball into a better scoring position.

Need to Move the Ball Fast? Join a Picket Line

One of the fastest way to move the ball from one end of the court to the other is with a picket line. What's that? It's a simple relay pattern in which four players space themselves along one side of the court, from beneath their opponents' basket to their own. Once the ball has been thrown inbounds in the backcourt, it's passed rapidly from player to player, with the goal being to score a basket quickly before the defense can get set up.

If done correctly (that is, with fast, accurate passes), a picket line is a fast, effective way to move the ball. And even if it doesn't result in an immediate basket, in a game with a shot clock it still increases the amount of time a team has to take a shot before the shot-clock buzzer goes off.

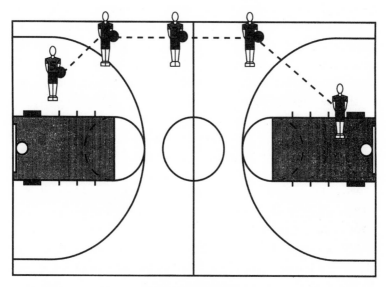

Picket line diagram

RECEIVING

It may seem silly to talk about receiving the ball as an important skill. After all, what we're really talking about is catching, and who doesn't know how to catch a ball? But there's a right way to receive a basketball, and a wrong way. So let's take a look at the difference.

The first thing you have to do when you're on the court is pay attention. This isn't the time to daydream or to recite all of the state capitals. Stay aware of what's going on around you, who has the ball, and where the defenders are on the court.

Let your teammates know that you want the ball by

keeping your eyes on the person who has it. Then, when a pass comes your way, step toward the ball (and, if possible, away from the player guarding you). Help out the passer by holding up one of your hands, palm facing out—what you're doing is making a target for the passer to throw the ball at.

It's important to relax. Don't stiffen your wrists and hands; keep them loose and flexible—it's called having *soft hands*. You want to cushion the ball with your hands, not have it bounce off them as if they were a wall.

Finally, once you've caught the ball, keep your body between it and the defensive player guarding you. That helps prevent a steal.

All of those things together make up the right way to receive a basketball. Now let's look at some wrong ways. Being caught by surprise when a pass comes your way (you should have been paying attention) will probably result in you fumbling the ball away. Or there's stepping away from the ball when it's passed to you (that's like moving a target just as someone shoots an arrow). Or there's having stiff hands or wrists, which makes the ball hard to hold on to, and makes it more likely that you'll lose control of it (or never have control in the first place).

To avoid these mistakes, practice your receiving skills. A good way to do this is to stand a few feet apart from a teammate and pass the ball back and forth a rapidly as you can. Not hard, just fast. You want to keep the ball under control. Fast passes force you to pay attention to the ball. Your goal is to stay focused on both your teammate and the ball, and to find a natural rhythm to what you're doing. That's what good passing and receiving depend on—players paying attention and working as a unit.

The Three-Man Weave

One way to work on your ball-handling skills is to run the three-man weave. You'll need (obviously) three players, plus a full-sized basketball court.

Start at one end of the court, with the three players spread an even distance apart. The player in the middle (Player 2) has the ball. As all three players begin running toward the other end of the court, here's what happens:

- *Player 2 bounce passes the ball to the player on his left (Player 1).*
- *Then Player 2 cuts behind Player 1, and Player 1 bounce passes the ball to the player on his right (Player 3).*
- *Player 1 cuts behind Player 3, and Player 3 bounce passes the ball to the player on his left (Player 2)*
- *And so forth, until they reach the other end of the court. Then turn around, passing and weaving back to the starting point.*

Don't worry if you have a hard time doing this at first. It takes time for the three players to learn how to adjust their speed and control their bounce passes so that the weave works properly. In a real game situation, a weave is a good way to break away from a tight defense while moving the ball rapidly down the court.

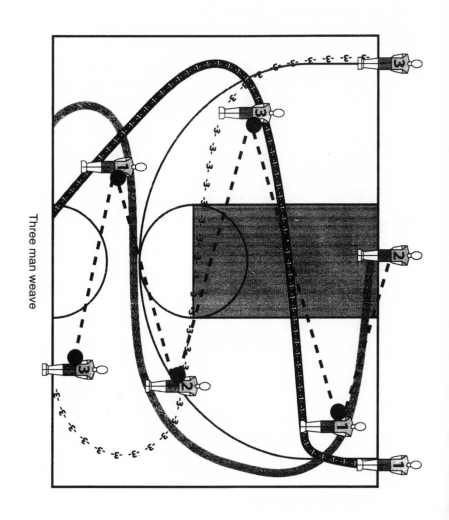

Three man weave

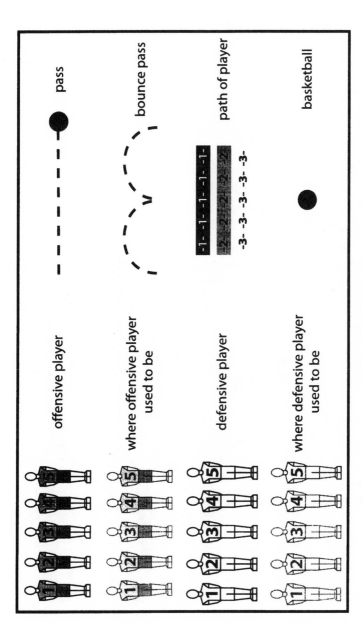

Key to diagrams

PIVOTING

At first, you might not think of the pivot as a ball-handling skill. Or as a skill at all, for that matter. After all, a pivot is just turning from side to side on one foot, right? Well, yes and no.

Yes, a pivot is turning from side to side on one foot. But no, that's not all there is to it. Learning to control your pivot will help you fake a move in one direction, then drive around a defender who moved out of position because of your fake. It will help you be able to move from having your back to the basket to a driving layup or a hook shot—that's called a reverse pivot. It will make you a harder player to guard effectively if you can pivot equally well in either direction.

Low and high post positions

The pivot is a crucial skill for any player who is playing in either the *low post* or the *high post*. The post is the portion of the court outside the foul lane, on either side, and below the free throw line. The low post is the area closest to the basket; the high post is farther away, on each end of the free throw line. Players who position themselves in these areas are said to be *posting up*. The pivot is important to them because they stand with their backs to the basket, and have to be able to pivot to one side or the other to shoot or pass the ball to teammates driving toward the basket.

The basic pivot is simple. With the ball in your possession, plant your left foot. That's your pivot foot—and you cannot move it. Now practice turning to your left, then your right. Think of your pivot foot as a door hinge: it allows you to swing from side to side, but it stays in one place. Now switch to your right foot, and pivot in both directions.

You might feel a little awkward at first. But the more you practice pivoting, the more comfortable you'll become. Have someone pass the ball to you, and practice pivoting in each direction.

Once you feel comfortable, practice a reverse pivot. With your back to the basket, catch the ball, plant your left foot, fake a pivot to the right, then pivot to the left and drive to the basket for a right-handed layup. Then try it by planting your right foot, faking to your left, and pivoting to your right for a left-handed layup.

A player who can pivot well can keep the ball from defenders, pass it to teammates, and create shots. Mastering the pivot will give you more control of the ball, and more control of yourself on the court.

Pivoting

HUSTLE, MUSCLE, AND JUMP: REBOUNDING'S BASICS

A rebound is what a shot becomes when it misses the basket: a loose ball bouncing off the basket or rim that offensive and defensive players try to grab. There's something thrilling about watching a good rebounder work the boards, pulling down the ball and either putting it back up (for offensive rebounds) or passing it downcourt (for defensive rebounds). But while you might think of rebounding as a skill only for tall players, in fact it's a skill that every player needs to develop.

Why? Because good rebounding can make the difference in a close game. In fact, the team that *controls the boards* (gets the most rebounds on both ends of the court) is usually the one that wins a game. And a team with several players who are skillful rebounders is one that poses a threat to all its opponents.

But let's face it: rebounding isn't glamorous. Nor is it easy. It requires that you be willing to bump and be bumped as you struggle for the ball underneath the basket. It requires that you scramble for the ball if it hits the floor. It requires that you be determined to get the ball no matter how many other opposing players want it, too.

Rebounding relies on getting close enough to the goal, being able to jump up at the right time to rebound the ball, and being determined to get and hold on to the ball. That means you might end up getting knocked around a little in the scramble for the ball, but it's all part of the game.

The first thing you have to learn to do is to be in the right place at the right time. You do so by putting yourself between the person guarding you and the basket. This means you've got the edge when it comes to going up for the ball—your defender is going to have to reach over your back and run the risk of fouling you.

But remember—you'll also be risking a foul if you start pushing and shoving other players under the basket. Getting into a good position for a rebound requires some hustle (and maybe a little muscle), but it never requires deliberately hurting someone.

Don't just stand in one place under the basket. For one thing, if you're on offense and you're standing in the foul lane, you'll be called for a three-second violation. Also, if you stand in one place, your opponents can get between you and the basket (this is called *boxing out*). Make sure you move around, whether you're on offense or defense, as you get into position for a rebound.

When you jump up for a rebound, keep your eye on the ball so you know how fast it's coming down and what direction it's going. Then, once you get the ball, hold on to it with both hands—unless you're tipping it back into the basket or to a teammate. By grabbing the ball and holding it in two hands, you make it hard for a player from the other team to snatch it away from you. You also have more control than if you try to scoop it away from the backboard with just one hand.

Once you've made your jump and gotten the rebound, stay low. Keep your back to defensive players if you can, and don't start dribbling or try to pass the ball until you have some clear space around you. Once you do, get the ball back into play, either for another shot if it was an offensive rebound or up the court if it was a defensive rebound.

Rebounding definitely takes practice. Offer to rebound when other players are shooting baskets. Work on making your jumps at just the right time, on grabbing the ball with two hands, and on protecting the ball when you get a rebound. Ask someone to guard you when you're rebounding so you can practice keeping the ball away from a defender.

Rebounding takes strong leg muscles (for jumping) and strong arm and shoulder muscles (for grabbing and holding on to the ball). That's when running and doing your push-ups and pull-ups will help. It also takes good eye–hand coordination—that's the ability to do the right thing at the right time because your hands respond to what your eyes are seeing.

A good way to practice your eye–hand coordination is to get a few friends together and form a line along one side of the foul line. Stand about three feet away from the backboard. The first person in line throws the ball up against the backboard, to the side of the basket, then runs to the back of the line. At the same time, the second person in line jumps, catches the ball, and throws it back up against the backboard. The third person in line does the same thing, and so on.

The idea is to keep catching the ball and putting it back up against the backboard without missing it. No one is trying to make a basket. This is a way to practice keeping your eye on the ball, jumping and catching it at the right time, and putting it back up.

It's hard work, but it pays off in two ways. If you're pulling down rebounds after the other team has missed shots, it means you're denying your opponents additional chances to score. If you're pulling down rebounds after your team has missed shots, it means you're giving your teammates additional chances to score. Either way, you're making a valuable contribution to your team's efforts.

In the process, you'll discover that you're capable of working hard on behalf of your team—that you're capable of being tougher, stronger, and more determined than you might have ever imagined. It's another step on the road to becoming a well-rounded team player. That's another one of rebounding's benefits: it builds character.

PRACTICE MAKES PERFECT

There's an old saying you've probably heard before: "Practice makes perfect." That's certainly true when it comes to ball-handling skills. The more you practice them, the nearer to perfection you'll be.

But not even the best players are perfect. What makes them as good as they are is the fact that they continue to work on their ball-handling skills. If you do the same, you'll find yourself being more comfortable whenever you have a basketball in your hands—you'll know what to do with it, and how to do it. That's called confidence. It's as close to perfection as anyone ever gets.

Chapter 6

NO HOTDOGS ALLOWED: SHOOTING FUN-DAMENTALS

Let's face it: while dribbling and passing skills may be the basis of playing good basketball, shooting baskets is where the fun is. After all, what player doesn't dream of sinking the game-winning three-pointer at the buzzer to win the NBA Finals?

But in reality, shooting is less about dreaming and more about doing. Learning to shoot well requires the same thing that any other skill, on or off the court, requires—practice. To become a good shooter, you have to shoot baskets and shoot baskets and shoot baskets. Then you have to shoot some more baskets.

And the baskets you're shooting should consist of the basic shots—layups, jump shots, hook shots, and free throws—that are the heart of good offense, not the slam dunks and half-court glory shots that you sometimes see in professional games. Even at that level, most of the points are scored by players who rely on the basics—layups, jump shots, hook shots, and foul shots. Do the same, and you'll find yourself scoring more often than the hotdogs who think that showing off is more important than making baskets.

GETTING IN TOUCH WITH THE TOUCH

Often you'll hear coaches or sports reporters talking about a player's "touch" as a shooter. What is a touch? It's the amount of control a player has over the ball when taking shots. Developing a shooting touch relies on ball release, shooting motion, the amount of arch and spin that you put on the ball, and using your legs to help you shoot. To get the touch, you should work on:

- **Ball release** How you release the ball affects whether or not it goes into the basket—or even gets close. A good release begins with the proper grip.

  Whether you're right-handed or left-handed, the hand you use the most is your *strong hand*. Your other hand is your *weak hand*. When you hold a basketball in your strong hand, spread your fingers so you can control the ball. Instead of gripping it tightly, let it rest in the palm of your strong hand while supporting it with your weak hand. To shoot, bend your wrist so your fingers are pointing up, raise your arm above your head with your elbow bent, snap your wrist, and release the ball with your fingertips.

  If you've done this properly, the ball will spin through the air. Follow through with your arm: the fingers of your shooting hand should be slightly curved and pointing toward the basket.

  Great shooters can shoot with either hand. So you also need to practice your ball release with your off hand. Being able to control and shoot with both hands will make you twice as hard to guard—and twice as likely to score.

- **Shooting motion** Good shooters are like acrobats: their bodies seem to glide automatically through every move. Developing that ability starts with a good ball release, but it also depends on having a good aim. That means you know exactly where you want the ball to go before you let go of it, and you shoot to hit that spot. Then you do what you can to make that happen: you jump high enough to get the shot off and you follow through after you've released the ball. You have to train your body to make the right moves.

- **Arch and spin** There's nothing prettier in basketball than watching a perfectly spinning ball arch through the air and into the basket. A good shooter makes it look so easy. The truth is, it's not that hard. It just takes practice. (But by now that shouldn't surprise you!)

  Releasing the ball with your fingertips will put a natural spin on the ball—and releasing it with your wrist at the proper angle will give it arch. The farther back you cock your wrist before releasing the ball, the higher the arch will be.

  Why is arching the ball important? Because it gives you more control over your shots, and a better chance of making the shots you take. It also allows you to shoot over tall opponents.

  To practice getting a high arch on your shots, have someone stand a couple of feet away from you and wave a broom in the air. The broom represents a tall player who's just waiting to smack one of your shots away—or to snatch it out of the air for a steal. Your job is to arch your shots over the broom. (This was an exercise that former Notre Dame coach Digger Phelps used with his players.)

Another skill you need to develop is putting spin on the ball: in fact, it's one of the most important skills you can develop as a shooter. And you can practice anytime you have a ball and some time on your hands. Practice cocking your wrist, snapping it forward, and releasing the ball with your fingertips. Do it with each hand. If you're doing it properly, the ball will spin through the air like a trapeze artist.

- **Use your legs to help you shoot** Legs? What do legs have to do with shooting a basketball? A lot. Legs are much stronger than arms. After all, your legs have to hold up your entire body: use that strength to help you shoot.

  When shooting, bend your knees and use the power of your legs to push your body up into the air. Think of your legs as springs that give you the extra burst of strength you need to propel your shots through the air. What happens when you push down on a spring? The coils tighten up. What happens when you release the spring? *Spoing!* The coils suddenly release all the energy that was created when you pushed them down. Your legs are like the coils in a spring. Use their strength and energy.

  When you're jumping into the air to take a shot, both feet can (and should) leave the ground. Release the ball at the top of your jump. Just remember that when you leave the ground with the ball, you have to get rid of it before you come back down, or you'll be called for up-and-down (the vertical version of traveling).

Your goal as a shooter is to practice your release, shooting motion, arch and spin, and leg movements so that you can do them all together, and do them without thinking about what you're doing. Great shooters do what they do as naturally as breathing.

THE LAYUP

One of the simplest shots, the layup is also one of the easiest to make consistently if you get in position. The best way to get started is to stand a couple of steps back from the basket, either to the right or left. You should be at an angle to the basket, not directly in front of it.

Now take one step and jump up, using one hand to lay the basketball up against the backboard. Shoot overhand, and aim for the square above the basket. If you're on the right side of the basket, use your right hand, raise your right knee, and push off the floor with your left foot. If you're on the left side of the basket, use your left hand, raise your left knee, and push off the floor with your right foot.

One way to remember the proper layup motion is to think of it as climbing a ladder. When you get close enough to the basket for your shot, start climbing the ladder by raising your outside knee and reaching up with your outside arm and hand. Then jump and release the ball against the backboard. (Not something you would normally do if you were climbing a ladder!)

Just as you should be able to dribble with either hand, you should be able to make layups from either side of the basket. Practice until you can. That way, no matter where you are on the floor, you'll be ready to drive for a layup. Or pivot.

Shooting the layup

Pivot? Layup? That's Mikan's Drill, named for NBA legend George Mikan, who played for the Minneapolis Lakers from 1949 to 1956. The drill was created by a coach at DePaul University where Mikan went to college, to help the young center improve his ability to pivot and lay the ball up accurately. It can do the same thing for you. Here's what you do:

- Stand under the basket with your back to the base-line.
- Holding the ball with both hands, pivot to your left and shoot a layup with your right hand. Remember to use the backboard. Catch the ball when it comes back down.
- Get back under the basket with your back to the baseline.
- Pivot to your right this time, and shoot a layup with your left hand. Use the backboard. Catch the ball as it comes back down.
- Do this exercise ten times on each side (ten right-handed layups and ten left-handed ones). Once you can do the drill well on both sides, try the power version: do the same thing going to each side as fast as you can. Shoot until you can make ten shots in a row (both sides combined).

After you've practiced layups from close in to the basket, gradually move back. Your goal is to be able to make a layup by driving toward the basket, dribbling until you're close enough (about two steps away) to lay up the ball. Keep your dribble low to help you control the ball. Keep your head up so you can see where you're going and when you get there.

Remember to use the backboard to guide the ball into the basket. Pick the spot you want to hit when you release the ball, and try to hit it. Control the speed of the ball—if you hit the backboard too hard, the ball will bounce off it instead of into the basket.

Once you're confident in your ability to shoot layups from both sides of the basket, have someone guard you as you drive for the basket. Work on using your speed and

your dribbling skill to beat the defender to the basket—
you can't go through that person, but you can go around.

Don't make the mistake of assuming you're going to
make a layup before you even shoot it! If you do, you're
less likely to pay attention to what you're doing—and
that's a mistake. You should always focus on your shots,
layups or not. Follow through on every shot, and be
ready for a rebound if necessary.

The layup is an important shot to any player in the low
or high post. In the low post you should be able to catch a
pass, pivot, take a step or two, and lay the ball up against
the backboard for a basket. In the high post you should
be able to catch a pass, pivot, and drive down the free
throw lane for a layup. In each case, being able to shoot
from either side of the basket doubles your chances for
scoring.

Some players consider layups easy shots, and they
make fun of anyone who spends too much time practicing
them. If that happens to you, ignore the jokes and work
on your layups. All it takes is one missed layup during a
game to point out why practice is so important.

THE JUMP SHOT

It's hard to imagine a basketball game in which the
players don't shoot jump shots. But until the 1960s, most
players kept at least one foot on the floor when shooting.
Leaping into the air while shooting was something very
few players did.

Today, being able to shoot jump shots is an important
skill for every player. Whether you're a forward only a
few feet from the basket or a guard out in three-point ter-

Jump shot

ritory, having a good jump shot makes you a valuable offensive player.

There are four basic areas you should practice taking jump shots from:

- **The elbows** The spots on the floor where, if the free throw line were longer, it would meet the edges of the circle at the top of the lane.

- **The right and left wings**   The spots halfway between the elbows and the baseline.
- **The right or left corners**   The places where the baseline meets the sidelines.
- **The top of the key**   The area on the floor at the edge of the three-point arc.

Hitting a jump shot from any of these places on the court depends on your shooting technique. Start by holding the ball a little above your head, with your shooting hand under it and your other hand steadying the ball from the side. Then jump straight up into the air as high as you can, aim for a point on the rim (or the backboard, if you're going to bank the ball into the basket), and release the ball.

How you release the ball is important. Your shooting hand should push the ball into the air, with a flick of the wrist, while your support hand should fall away without doing anything to the ball. Don't forget to put an arch on the ball instead of shooting straight at the rim (which is called *shooting a brick*). If the ball arches up into the air, it's harder for a defensive player to intercept, and it's less likely to bounce off the rim.

Remember, the basket is eighteen inches in diameter—and a basketball is nine inches. So accuracy is important. Don't be afraid to use the backboard. While you might think that arcing a shot into the basket looks great, a shot that banks off the backboard (it's called a *bankshot*) is worth just as many points.

In fact, for many years the bankshot was a favorite of basketball players. Though not as flashy as a shot that just swishes through the net, it's often more accurate. Just aim for the square on the backboard.

After you take a shot, don't stand around admiring it. You need to follow through—move toward the basket and keep your eye on the ball. Try to get into position for a rebound, just in case your shot misses.

To develop your jump shot, practice shooting from different places on the court. Take several shots (start with ten or twenty, and gradually increase the number to one hundred) from each place. Work on your jump, your release, and your follow-through. Be patient. You have to train your body so that shooting jump shots is part of its natural rhythm on the court, and that takes time.

You'll probably miss more shots than you make at first, but don't get discouraged. Some players master jump shots—or other types of shots, for that matter—faster than other players. But it's not how long it takes that matters: it's how determined you are to succeed, and how willing you are to put in the time and effort it takes to do it. Eventually your shots will feel right to you, and you'll find yourself making more than you miss.

THE HOOK SHOT

One of the greatest hook shot masters of all time was Kareem Abdul-Jabbar. At seven feet, two inches tall, Abdul-Jabbar had height on his side—and he also had long arms. Those traits allowed him to arch the ball high in the air, which led to the shot being called the *sky hook*.

What Abdul-Jabbar was shooting, however, was just a slightly modified version of the basic hook shot. Although many people think of the hook shot as something that the center does, any player can learn to shoot it—and should. All games involve action close to the basket, and

knowing how to shoot a hook shot will give you another
way to score in those circumstances.

Because a hook shot is an inside shot (that is, it's
taken close to the basket), practice it from just a few feet
away—the low post position, for example. Start with
your back to the basket and turn to one side or the other.
If you turn to the right, hold the ball against your right

Hook shot

side, bring it up with your right hand, and take a step or make a small jump, pushing off with your left foot. Swing your right arm up, releasing the ball when it's at its highest point above your head. Aim for the spot on the rim that's closest to you.

Practice taking hook shots with each hand, and from different distances. But stay inside the foul line—it's rare that anyone takes a hook shot out past it. Why? Because the hook shot is an inside shot: it's hard to take an accurate hook shot if you're more than ten or twelve feet from the basket. Hook shots are harder to do than layups, but just as important to your development of an inside game.

The Free Throw (or Foul Shot)

A free throw (or foul shot) is the free shot that you get if you're on offense and a referee decides that a player from the other team has fouled you. You take the shot from the free throw line nearest your goal.

Coaches consider the free throw the most important shot that their players take: each free throw is an opportunity to put one uncontested point on the scoreboard. That's why there's nothing more frustrating to a coach (not to mention a player or a fan) than a missed free throw. One or two or three missed shots add up fast, especially in a close game when those missed shots mean that one or two or three points don't go on the scoreboard. Sometimes this can mean the difference between winning and losing a game.

While everyone misses a free throw now and then, consistently poor shooting is usually the result of bad form (how a player shoots the shot), not enough practice, or both. The only way to have good form as a free throw shooter, however, is to practice: that means if you solve one problem, you solve both.

When it comes to form, think of a foul shot as a jump shot—without the jump. When you're shooting a free throw, your feet must remain on the floor, which makes shooting a free throw a lot like taking an old-fashioned shot called a *set shot*—a shot in which a player keeps his or her feet planted while shooting with one or both hands.

In the case of a free throw, the important thing is to bend your knees as you prepare to shoot. Bring the ball up so it's slightly above your head, with your shooting hand on top of it and your other hand steadying it underneath. Using your legs like springs, push the ball up and release it, aiming it at the square painted on the backboard. Raise up on your toes and stretch your arms out as you release the ball.

The key to successful free throw shooting is to relax. Tune out any noise around you. Focus on the basket, and on the fact that you can put the ball in it. If you get anxious, you're more likely to miss. But if you relax and focus, you'll find you make more than you miss.

Assuming, of course, that you (let's hear it, class) *practice*. Every time you're on the court or playground, shoot some free throws. Work on getting a feel for what works best for you. The more shots you take, the more confident you'll become. And confidence is an important part of becoming a good shooter, whether you're at the free throw line, in the low post, or out in three-point territory.

Free throw

Shooting Games

Working on shooting is important, but it doesn't have to be boring. There are some games you can play that will give you the practice you need while keeping you entertained.

Take H-O-R-S-E, for instance. You probably know how to play this game already—you shoot the ball from anyplace on the court. If the shot is good, all the other players in the game have to take the same shot from the same place. Anyone who misses gets a letter—the first miss is H, the second is O, and so on, until someone has H-O-R-S-E and is out of the game. The last player left is the winner.

This is a good game for practicing your shots. Start with layups or foul shots, then begin using other shots—jumpers from different distances, a hook shot, shots using your "weak" hand (the left if you're right-handed, the right if you're left-handed).

Then there's Around the World, another game you're probably familiar with. You start by shooting a layup on the right side of the basket, then work your way around to the left side by making shots from different spots on the court—the right baseline corner, the right corner of the foul lane, the top of the key, the foul line, the left corner of the foul lane, the left corner of the baseline, and a layup from the left side of the basket.

Every time you make a shot, you move to the next spot on the corner and take that shot. When you miss a shot, you stay where you are until your next turn. The first player to make it all the way "around the world" (from one side of the basket to the other and back) wins. This is a great game for practicing both inside (close to the basket) and outside (away from the basket) shots.

Of course, you can always make up your own games as well. See how many shots you can hit from the same spot on the court. Or take a certain number of layups, jump shots, hook shots, and foul shots (say, ten to twenty-five of each) and keep track of how many of each you make every day for a month.

And get some of your friends together to play basketball games as often as possible. There's no better way to learn how to shoot in a game than to play in a game. While it might not be exactly like playing in a league or school game, it will give you practice in shooting—and many other skills as well.

SHOT SELECTION

Part of becoming a confident shooter is knowing when to shoot and when not to shoot. And that comes with experience. Don't be afraid to shoot just because there's a defensive player close by—if you know you can hit the shot you're taking.

For instance, if you're being guarded but you know you can hit a short jump shot just by taking a step back and arching your shot over the defender's head, do it. But if that defender is sticking closely to you and making it hard for you to catch a pass, let alone take a shot, don't try to dribble past for a layup. Unless, of course, you don't mind the ball being stolen from you.

Learn to choose your shots carefully. A good shooter doesn't shoot every time he or she touches the ball. A good shooter knows when the time is right, and takes shots that have a good chance of going in. That's called getting good *looks* at the basket. Once in a while you might have to take a "miracle" shot (there's three seconds left and your team's down by one point, for example), but the rest of the time you shouldn't have to pray for your shots to hit the hoop.

Some other no-nos for shooters: Don't take a shot when you're tired or you're fumbling the ball. Don't take a shot you've never tried before. Don't take a shot if none of your teammates is around to rebound.

Speaking of your teammates, never take a shot when one of them is open for a better one. Don't forget that basketball is a team sport, and you need your teammates' help on the court, just as they need your help. If you start taking bad shots when other players are open for good ones, you'll get a reputation as a ball hog—someone who has forgotten the importance of teamwork. Remember, bad shots give your opponents new opportunities to score.

A good shooter knows that working with his or her teammates benefits everyone. Someone who regularly gets passes from you is going to return the favor. And receiving good passes at the right times leads to good shots. That's all the more reason to work on your shooting. Making sure that your skills are sharp gives you an edge on the court; it prepares you to make the best of every shooting opportunity that comes your way—whether it's lots of looks in a game or just a few.

It's not how often you take a shot that counts: it's how

good the shots are that you take. The best shooters practice constantly so that when they get a shot opportunity, they have a good chance of making it count.

The Discovery of Three-Point Land

Three-point shots are so much a part of modern basketball that you might not realize they haven't always been part of the sport. In fact, the first three-pointer in the NBA occurred on October 12, 1979, when Boston Celtics player Chris Ford hit one in the first quarter of a game against the Houston Rockets. A shot that once would have put only two points on the scoreboard for the Celtics was suddenly worth three.

But that wasn't the first three-pointer in basketball history. The three-point shot was a regular part of American Basketball League (1961–62) and American Basketball Association (1967–76) games. And it made its first appearance in a college game in 1945— though it never caught on and wasn't used again until 1980.

November 29, 1980, to be precise, in a game between Western Carolina State College and Middle Tennessee State College. Western Carolina player Ronnie Carr got the honor: he hit a twenty-three-footer from the left corner. The ball that he used, plus a photo and a videotape of the shot, are in the Basketball Hall of Fame in Springfield, Massachusetts.

Chapter 7

WHICH BASKET'S OURS? A FEW TIPS ON PLAYING OFFENSE

Pick and roll. Give and go. Alley-oop. From playgrounds to the pros, moves like those are what makes basketball exciting to play—and watch. They're also what separates team-based basketball from run-and-gun games at recess.

Despite the superstar players who get all the attention, basketball is a team sport. That's especially true on offense. The offensive team is the one with the ball, the one trying to score. It's five players trying to play as one unit.

How do they do that? Simple. Through teamwork.

Teamwork consists of individual players combining their skills to achieve a common goal: making more baskets than their opponents. That's the goal of any team's offense.

A BASKETBALL COURT IS NO PLACE FOR DAYDREAMING

Hey! Wake up! Pay attention! Teamwork begins with five alert players. There's nothing more embarrassing than fumbling a pass or turning the ball over because

128

you weren't paying attention. But it's surprisingly easy to do.

Sometimes during a game, your mind might wander, especially if you're tired or distracted by a problem (maybe a homework assignment or an argument with a friend). At those times the best thing you can do is force yourself to concentrate on what's happening right at that moment. Make your mind focus on the present.

Once the game is over, you can turn your attention to other things. Like what clothes to wear for the field trip on Friday or how long the longest river in the world actually is.

THE TIP-OFF SENDS A MESSAGE

How many times have you seen a game-opening tip-off treated like it didn't matter? It seems to happen a lot in NBA games, where the attitude often appears to be, "We don't care if we get the tip or not."

That's not smart basketball. The team that gets the ball first has the opportunity to score first. But more important, it has the opportunity to take control of the game. By snatching the ball at tip-off, a team delivers a message to its opponent: *We came to win.* That's a strategic advantage.

A smart player (and a smart team) steps on the court ready to play the game as well and as hard as possible. That starts by taking the tip-off seriously. If you're tipping for your team, be prepared to jump as high as you can. Tip the ball toward the teammate who's calling the plays. Then get into position for a shot or a rebound.

If you're not tipping, then position yourself somewhere

outside the circle and be ready to catch the ball if it comes your way. Once the tip has happened, get into position to run the offensive play that your coach has called.

Of course, if your team lost the tip, set up your defense immediately. There's no time to waste—you have to keep the other team from scoring. Just because your team didn't get the tip doesn't mean you're in trouble—but you will be if you let your opponents score at will.

Oh, and make sure you know which basket is your team's *before the tip-off*. If you're not sure, ask the referee. You don't want to get the tip, then score on the wrong end of the court! (Sometimes players forget or don't pay attention when the referee indicates which basket belongs to which team, so don't think it can't happen to you.)

PLAYING AROUND

Every basketball team has a series of *plays* that it uses to try to beat the defense and score. A play is a planned set of moves among teammates, who are in various places on the court; it's designed to create a shot for one of the players by outsmarting or outmaneuvering the defensive players.

Developing plays is a coach's responsibility. Putting them into action is the players'. That's what makes practice sessions so crucial. A team's offensive plan only works when everyone on the team knows what's supposed to happen in every play—for instance, whether a play sets up the shooting guard to take a three-point shot or the small forward to drive inside for a layup. You have to know where you're supposed to be at all times, and what you're supposed to be doing to help make the play work—even if that's just staying out of the way of two other players who are involved in the play.

That's why college and professional teams provide players with *playbooks*—notebooks filled with diagrams and explanations of each play. Players are expected to study their playbooks, and know precisely what they're supposed to do on the court with each play. In other words, they have homework to do: it's part of learning to play basketball well.

While that might seem difficult if you're more used to running around on the court than to running plays, it really isn't. Most plays consist of a few basic things: passes, screens and picks, and locations on the court.

The Greatest Offensive Player in History?

Anytime you start attaching the label greatest *to anyone, you run the risk of starting an argument. In basketball, as in every other sport, coaches, players, sportswriters, and fans all have their opinions about which player was (or is) the greatest at this or that. But it's hard to argue with the facts when it comes to Wilt "The Stilt" Chamberlain, whom many sportswriters and historians consider the greatest all-around basketball player in history.*

Chamberlain, whose NBA career spanned 1959 to 1973, was a seven-foot, one-inch basketball wizard who scored a record hundred points in a single NBA game in 1962, a feat no one has matched since. That's the same year that he averaged more than fifty points per game, tallied more than four thousand

*points for the season, and played nearly every minute
of every game for his team, the Philadelphia 76ers.*

*But Chamberlain was more than just a great scorer.
He was also a skillful rebounder, once pulling down
fifty-five rebounds in one game. He also led the NBA is
assists during the 1968–69 season, with a record 702!*

*While there have been many talented offensive
players throughout basketball's long history, Chamberlain is often ranked at the top for his dedication to
playing the game as well as any player ever has.*

NEVER PASS UP A GOOD PASS

You've probably played basketball with players who
never pass—or, as they're often known, "ball hogs." Ball
hogs don't make good teammates. Good teammates pass
the ball to one another, and look for ways to help one another look good on the court. Ball hogs think there's no
glory in giving the ball to someone else. They want to be
the center of attention, which to them means having the
ball as much, and for as long, as possible.

They're right about one thing: ball hogs are the center
of attention. The defensive team's center of attention!
With a ball hog holding on to the ball, the defenders know
right where to concentrate their efforts. Forget about the
other four offensive players—with a ball hog on the court,
they won't touch the ball often enough to be a threat.

But a team that knows the power of passing is a team
that's hard to beat. That's because passes help create
scoring opportunities for offensive players.

When you're on the court, stay alert. If you've got the

ball, look for a teammate who's in a good position for a pass. And if you don't have the ball, look for chances to shake free of your defender and get yourself open to catch a pass. Whether you're passing or receiving, never pass up a good pass.

SCREENS AREN'T JUST FOR WINDOWS

In basketball, a screen doesn't keep out the bugs. But it does interfere with those pesky defensive players. A screen is a move made by one offensive player to help a teammate get away from a defender and receive a pass or take a shot. To set a screen, an offensive player steps behind or beside a defensive player, blocking that player from guarding another offensive player.

Learning to set a screen is simple. Ask three friends to help you. Player 1 has the ball. Player 2 guards Player 3. You set a screen by standing behind or next to Player 2. That allows Player 3 to run past or behind you, and catch a pass from Player 1.

The important thing to remember about setting a screen is this: once you do it, you can't move. You must stand in one place without touching the defensive player. A moving screen is illegal.

PICKING AND GRINNING

Miners use one type of pick, guitar players use another. But a pick in basketball isn't like either of them. In basketball, a pick is a screen that's set to help the player who has the ball get away from his defender.

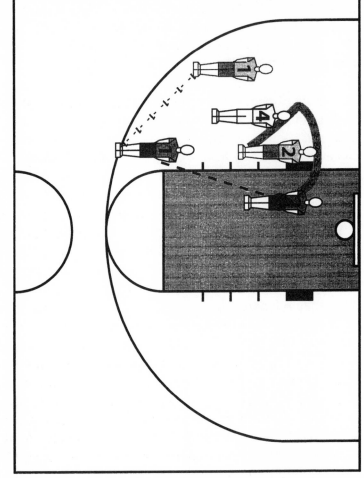

Pick and roll play

The *pick and roll* is one of basketball's most basic—and most effective—plays. Offensive Player 1 sets a pick on the defender who's guarding Offensive Player 2. Player 2 has the ball. After setting the pick, Player 1 moves *(rolls)* away from the defender, often toward the basket. Then Player 2 has the option of shooting, with Player 1 there for the rebound, or passing to Player 1, who shoots the ball.

To practice the pick and roll, you'll need two friends—one on defense, the other on offense. The offensive player has the ball: you set the pick on the defensive player. Setting a pick is just like setting a screen. Remember, no touching! And once again, you can't move—a moving pick is against the rules.

After you've set the pick, the player with the ball "rolls" away from the defender, either toward the basket or to the outside. If she rolls in toward the basket, you follow for a rebound. If she rolls outside, you head for the basket to rebound if she takes an outside shot—or to catch a pass from her and shoot a layup.

To make a pick and roll work, you and your teammate have to be aware of each other. You have to know where your teammate goes when she rolls off your pick—and she has to know where you go once the pick is done. That's why you need to practice different options, so when you're in an actual game, everyone will know what to do and where to go on the court. Otherwise, someone will end up passing to a spot where a teammate should be, only to discover too late that there's no one there. The result? An interception or a turnover.

When it's done well, a pick and roll results in an easy basket—and grins on the faces of the team that scores (and its fans). That's worth practicing for.

GIVE AND GO

Another play that's as much fun as a pick and roll is the *give and go*. It's used when a defensive player isn't paying close enough attention—which means that player is easy to beat to the basket.

Give and go is easy to execute—and hard to defend against once it's under way. What happens is that two offensive players (1 and 2) work together to fool the defensive player guarding Player 1.

Try it for yourself. You'll need two friends. You're Offensive Player 1, one friend is Offensive Player 2, and the other friend is guarding you. You're inside, near the basket, and you have the ball. Pass it out to Player 2, then run out beyond the free throw line. When the defender follows you, cut back inside toward the basket. Player 2 then bounce passes the ball to you, and you shoot a short jump shot or a layup. If you moved quickly enough, the defender is a few steps behind you and can't prevent your shot.

Speed is the key to the give and go. The player who's cutting toward the basket has to do it fast before the defender can react.

ALLEY-OOP

An *alley-oop* is a two-player action in which one player throws a high, arching pass close to the basket so a second player can jump up, catch the ball, and dunk it in the basket, all done in one continuous motion before coming down. A well-done alley-oop is a beautiful thing to see.

But it's not something that every player or every team

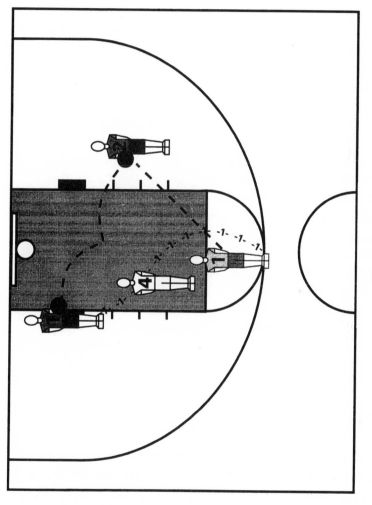

Give and go

can do well. Why? Because it relies on a perfectly timed pass and a player who's tall enough (or who can leap high enough) to jump up, snatch the high pass, and stuff it into the basket while still in the air. It's a crowd-pleasing type of play, bound to bring fans to their feet (spilling soft drinks and dumping popcorn boxes in the process).

An alley-oop is not a play for inexperienced players. Nor is it a play that should be used regularly. Usually it works best on a fast break, when the offensive team is able to move the ball downcourt quickly. The two players involved in setting up an alley-oop have to know what each one is going to do, then they have to run the play accurately. A bad pass or a jump too soon can ruin it.

That's why it's a good idea to stick to basic plays—pick and roll, give and go—and leave the fancy stuff to players who know what they're doing. (But it never hurts to try it out for fun when you're just shooting around with your friends. Just be careful.)

OFFENSIVE PLAYS

Creating the plays that a team is going to run is the coach's job. Learning to run those plays is the players' job. That's why coaches require every player to be at every practice session, unless there's a really good reason to miss one.

There are as many different kinds of offensive plays as there are coaches. A coach's play making is limited only by the fact that there are only five offensive players on the floor at a time—though a coach might have his players run one play, call a time-out, then substitute a player in the game to run a second play that's based on where the ball was on the court before the time-out.

Simple plays rely on two players to work together, usually by combining some passes and a screen or a pick. But other players put more players into action, including having all five involved. Regardless of the number of players that a play needs, your job as a player is to know where you're supposed to be on the court when the play is being run—and what you're supposed to do. Your teammates are counting on you.

In basketball, a good offense begins and ends with teamwork.

Going in the Back Door

One of the oldest and best-known offensive moves in basketball is the back-door play. It begins with an offensive player passing the ball to a teammate who's playing near the basket. Then the player who passed the ball (or another offensive player) pretends to cut away from the basket, faking defenders out of position, and cuts back toward the basket.

The player who received the pass then passes the ball to the teammate who's cutting inside, and that player shoots a layup. It's simple, effective, and—if all goes well—an easy basket. That's because a well-done back-door play is nearly impossible to stop once it's in motion.

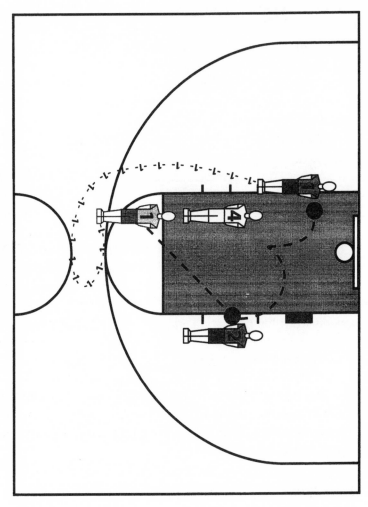

Back door play

Chapter 8

KEEP YOUR GUARD UP: LEARNING TO PLAY DEFENSE

In basketball most of the glory goes to great offensive players and plays—great dribbling, wicked passes, thrilling shots. But defense is what makes a game interesting. The ability of one team to put pressure on another, forcing bad shots or turnovers, keeps a game from being just a back-and-forth trade-off of baskets.

Playing defense is all about focus and effort. You have to be able to stay focused on the player you're guarding. Watch for habits—one player likes to dribble with one hand, but not the other; another player likes to shoot ten-foot jump shots, but not longer ones. Then interfere with those habits by moving to the dribbler's favorite side or by forcing the shooter outside ten-foot range.

You have to make the effort to play good defense. But if you can prevent easy baskets and force the offense to make mistakes, isn't it worth the effort? After all, a good defense can keep your team in a game, even if you aren't doing too well on offense.

THE DEFENSIVE STANCE

Have you ever seen a defensive player standing in front of an offensive player, waving his arms like a wind-

141

Correct defensive stance

mill? What happened? An alert offensive player probably faked to one side, making the defender lean in that direction, then drove in the opposite direction. The defender, caught off balance, couldn't recover in time to prevent the drive. That's an example of how *not* to play defense.

How should you play it? By crouching. Bend your knees slightly, feet about as far apart as your shoulders. Stay on the balls of your feet, so you can move easily. Keep your arms relaxed with palms facing forward, ready to move up or down to block shots or slap away careless dribbles. This is called the *defensive stance*. It's as important to learning how to play basketball well as dribbling or shooting layups. Maybe more important.

Why should you crouch instead of standing upright? It's a matter of balance. In a crouch you can move side to side or up and back without losing your balance. But when you stand straight up and lean to one side, you risk tipping over. That's why a good defender stays crouched most of the time.

When you move, make sure you move both feet. If you move only one foot, once again you risk being off balance. But if you move both feet, you have the ability to switch directions without wobbling around like a bowling pin.

Instead of lifting your feet all the way off the ground, you're going to shuffle quickly—as if you're sliding on a freshly waxed floor in your socks. Do this shuffle-stepping whether you're moving side to side, or forward and back. Never cross your feet.

To practice moving correctly, get in a crouch and extend your hands. Then have someone tell you when to move—and in what direction. "Forward! To your left! Backward!" And so on. Practice moving smoothly—and changing directions quickly.

You can do this with two or three friends. Think of it as a race. Use the foul lane on a court, and have someone keep time as you see who can move from one side of the lane to the other and back the most times in ten seconds. Your goal is to increase the number of times you move back and forth across the lane in the allotted time. You need to be able to move quickly on defense, and this drill gives you the chance to work on your speed. As you get better at moving fast, increase the time limit so you can work on increasing your endurance as well as improving your speed.

There's one exception to shuffle-stepping on defense, and that's if the player you're guarding is dribbling on the run and passes you. Then you have to do what's called a *turn and go*. This means that once your opponent has run past you, you turn and go—run as fast as you can past him. Once you're ahead again, turn and get back in the defensive stance.

The better balanced you are and the more smoothly you can move, the easier it will be for you to play defense. And the more effective you'll be, because offensive players won't be able to fake you out of position as easily as they can players who don't know how to stand or move.

USE YOUR HEAD

Playing defense well depends on your ability to use your head. Or, to put it another way, playing defense depends on your ability to pay attention to what the offensive player you're guarding is doing, then to think about how you should respond.

Thinking makes the difference between good defensive players and poor ones. Good defensive players don't act on impulse—they know what they're doing and why they're doing it. Poor defensive players merely react to something the offense does without thinking—and the result is often either easy offensive baskets or a string of careless defensive fouls.

When you're playing defense, consider how fast the player whom you're guarding can move. If that player is faster than you, what should you do? Think about it first. That's right, you should stay about a step or two back so when your opponent moves forward, you can move back easily and stay in your defensive stance.

Also, you should consider how well the player you're guarding can shoot. What are that player's favorite shots—right-handed layups, ten-foot jump shots, three-pointers from the corners? Pay attention, then think about what you should do. Got it? Right—stay close when the player's in position to shoot from a favorite spot. By staying close, you'll make it more difficult to get a shot off, and you'll increase the possibility that any shot taken will be off the mark because you've forced the shooter to take a hurried or desperate shot.

Finally, consider what skills the player you're guarding has trouble doing. Dribbling with the left hand? Shooting from beyond the free throw line? Passing accurately? Watch, learn, and think. Then do what you can to force your opponent to have to dribble left-handedly (crowd the right side), shoot from outside (play close inside, but allow some room outside), or pass (force a poor pass by edging your opponent into a corner).

Also, learn to *anticipate*. Once you recognize some of an opponent's strengths and weaknesses, you'll be able to anticipate what that player's likely to do on the court, whether it's heading for the free throw line for a jump shot or passing the ball to a player on the left while cutting to the right. Anticipation is a critical part of your basketball skills, and one that requires you to use your mind as well as your body on defense.

When you're playing defense, you have to *do* something: it's your job to prevent the player you're guarding from making a basket or helping another offensive player score. But don't just do *anything:* think about it first. The more you use your head, the less you'll have to worry about whether or not you're doing the right thing.

USE YOUR HANDS

So you're in your defensive crouch, and the offensive player you're supposed to be guarding shows up right in front of you. Now what? Remember that your main responsibility on defense is to prevent the offensive team from scoring. And the best way to do that is to use your hands.

On defense, your hands are the most important part of your game (aside from your head). If the player you're guarding doesn't have the ball, then it's your job to keep it that way. Put one hand in the air between your opponent and the ball at all times.

If the player you're guarding has the ball, then you have to decide what to do with your hands. Is that player dribbling? Spread your arms out and drop your hands low. Did your opponent just catch a pass? Put one hand in the player's face and the other on the side where the ball is. That way you're ready for either a pass or shot attempt.

To challenge a shot, raise your hands high. Don't try slapping at the ball unless you're sure you can hit it and not your opponent. Otherwise you might have prevented a successful shot only to give the offense one or two points from the foul line.

Learning to block shots takes practice and time. While it looks easy (all you have to do is slap the ball away, right?), it isn't. To do it well, and to stay out of foul trouble while doing it, try blocking a right-handed shot with your left hand. Or try jumping into the air to block the ball after it has been released, not while it's still in the shooter's hands. Remember, you can knock the ball out of flight if it's on it's way up, but not if its coming down toward the basket.

Also, pick up the player you're guarding as far from the offensive basket as you can. By keeping your opponent away from the basket and the other offensive players, you can force long or wild shots and passes—which you might just pick off. If you find yourself guarding a player who's close enough to the basket to take a shot, stand taller and be prepared to block the ball.

After you've been guarding a player for a while, you'll recognize that player's favorite shots and favorite places on the floor to take them. Then you can stop the shots by standing in those spots. It's simple, but effective. It's called "taking a player out of the game."

USE YOUR FEET

Footwork is an important part of playing defense. As a defensive player, your job is not to stand around watching the action going on around you. It's to move with that action—and with the player you're guarding. To do that, you need to be aware of your feet. Keep them moving. In the defensive stance, make sure you shuffle-step in any direction that the action takes you.

Never lean too far forward on your toes or backward on your heels. Why? Because you'll lose your balance—and the person you're guarding. An off-balance defensive player is easy to run past or around, and easy to beat to the basket.

Also, don't cross your feet when you're moving. If you do, you'll get them tangled up if your opponent switches direction. And you'll be left standing flat-footed when your opponent rockets past you to pass, score, or rebound.

USE YOUR MOUTH

Defense is a teamwork effort. It relies on players talking to each other, letting one another know what's going on. For example, if the player you're guarding has the ball and gets past you on a pick, yell out "Switch!" That lets your teammates know that the player you're guarding is free and someone needs to move over and guard him.

By the same token, if you hear one of your teammates calling for assistance and you're close by, move over to help. Do you see someone setting a pick? Call it so your teammate on whom it's being set has a chance to react. Has double-teaming one opponent left another good shooter open? It's time to shout out a warning. It's this type of teamwork that separates a strong defensive team from a weak one.

Remember, you can talk on the court. Not only can you talk, you *should* talk. Let your teammates know what's going on. Silence may be golden in places such as a library, but it can be deadly on the court. Players who don't tell one another what's happening aren't playing as a team. And they're probably not playing very effective defense either.

Strong Side, Weak Side

You'll often hear sportscasters talking about the strong side and the weak side of the court. The strong side is the side of the court where the ball is; the weak side is the opposite side. Obviously, on defense the strong side is where the action is, but this doesn't mean you should leave the weak side unguarded.

That's because, at any moment, the weak side can become the strong side. All it takes is a good pass or a quick offensive ball handler who spots an opening. The action shifts, and you'd better have some defenders on hand to keep the offense in check.

MAN-TO-MAN VERSUS ZONE DEFENSE

There are two basic types of defense: man-to-man (which in women's basketball is often called *player-to-player*) and zone. Some coaches favor one type over the other; some switch back and forth.

Man-to-man defense is exactly that: each defensive player guards one specific offensive player. For many basketball fans, it's the best kind of defense because it pits the skills of one player against the skills of another. For this reason, until the 2001–2002 season, it was the only kind of defense that was permitted in the NBA.

A zone defense divides the court into different areas (zones), and makes a defensive player responsible for a specific zone (or portion of a zone). The defender has to guard any offensive player who comes into that zone.

Zone defense often is played in high school and college games.

For many years, however, NBA officials believed that zone defenses slowed down games and shut down the shooters who attract fans. If a referee suspected a team of playing any type of zone defense, the team could be penalized for what was known as *illegal defense*. The result was a technical foul, which meant a free throw for the offense. But in the 2001–2002 season, league officials relented, and now zone defenses are part of NBA games, too.

There are different types of zone defenses. For instance, in a 2–3 zone, two players remain up in the foul-line area while three others stay down near the basket. Other zones have different numbers of players at different places on the court.

As a player, you have to play the type of defense that your team's coach prefers. This means that over several years of playing, you'll probably learn to play a variety of zone defenses as well as man-to-man. That's good: the more you learn about different defensive styles, the better you'll be as a defender in any situation.

PLAYING MAN-TO-MAN DEFENSE

The most important thing to remember when playing man-to-man defense is this: your job is to prevent the player you're guarding from scoring, rebounding, and helping other offensive players score. That's all there is to it.

When is an opposing player the biggest threat? When he has just gotten the ball. That's when anything is possible—from a quick pass to a teammate in a good shooting position to a quick shot off the dribble. Your job is to shut down these possibilities. Begin by assuming the defensive stance and keeping your eyes on your opponent.

That's harder than it sounds. By keeping your eyes on your opponent, you know where he is, but not what's he's going to do. Maybe he'll try faking a pass or jerking his head to one side to move you out of position. Don't move unless you see him actually move his body (not just his head).

Try to keep your body between your opponent and the basket. If he's dribbling the ball, try to force him to move toward the sideline or the baseline: you can do this by staying between him and any open space there might be on the court. Then keep edging him where you want him to go.

Also, watch for chances to steal the ball. If you've noticed that a player doesn't like to dribble with his left hand, crowd him on the right side. That will force him either to dribble with his weak hand or to dribble on the side closest to you. Either way, you've got a chance to slap the ball away.

Of course, if your opponent stops dribbling, you know that he can only pass or shoot. And the only movement he can make is with his pivot foot. If you've forced him close to the sideline or baseline, he doesn't have much room to work.

If he tries to pass the ball to a teammate, you've got a chance to knock it away or steal it. If he tries to shoot, you've got the chance to block it. Either way, you're in charge of the situation.

That's what you're always trying to do when you're playing man-to-man defense: take charge. As the defensive player, you want to be the one who determines what happens when your opponent has the ball. If you can force him to make a bad shot, try a poor pass, or turn the ball over—or if you've prevented your opponent from even touching the ball—you've done your job.

If there's one basic rule to remember when you're playing defense, it's this: never turn your back on the player you're guarding. If he has the ball, obviously he's going to take off around you and try to make a basket or pass to a teammate who's in position to shoot. If he doesn't have the ball, he's still going to take off around you, this time to try to get into position to receive a pass and shoot. Either way, turning your back on the offense is an invitation to disaster.

The Art of Stealing the Ball

One thing you need to learn to do as a defensive player is how to steal the ball from your opponent. The key to successful steals is to catch the ball handler unaware. This means you have to be especially alert so that if an opportunity to steal the ball comes your way, you're ready.

Your best chances for steals usually come when:

- *An offensive player makes a sloppy pass—an across-court bounce pass, for instance, that you can snatch off the bounce, or a long high pass that you can intercept.*
- *An offensive player tries to dribble between you and another defender. Take a step or two and edge the offensive player toward your teammate. Then watch for a desperation move—a crossover dribble to a weak hand or a hasty attempt to pass the ball—and make your move.*

- *An offensive player seems confused about where to be on the court. If that player gets the ball, you might have a chance to grab a bad pass or block (then recover) a weak shot.*

PLAYING ZONE DEFENSE

Why do some coaches choose to play zone defense while others prefer man-to-man? Sometimes it depends on the situation. For example, if a coach knows that the opposing team is particularly good at inside shooting, but not so good from the outside, he or she might decide to use a zone that makes it harder to take inside shots.

For example, one of the most popular types of zone defenses is called a *2–3 zone*. This means that there are two defenders in the area on each side of the foul line, and three defenders closer to the basket.

In this type of zone pattern, the two outside defenders are responsible for defending against outside shots (also known as *perimeter shots*), while the three inside defenders are responsible for defending against layups, hook shots, and inside jumpers.

One of the most important things that you have to remember as a defensive player in a 2–3 zone (or any zone, for that matter) is to *keep your hands up!* Why is this so crucial? Think about it for a minute. If you're an offensive player with the ball and you're facing ten hands waggling in the air, ready to snatch the ball out of the air, making a pass is going to be hard to do.

In addition to the 2–3 zone, there are 1–3–1 and 1–2–2 zones. The first number in a zone sequence always refers to the number of defenders farthest from the basket, and

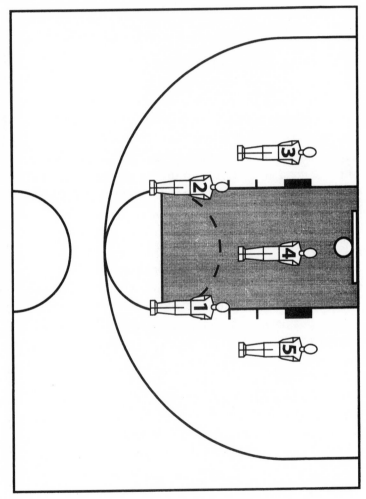

2–3 zone defense

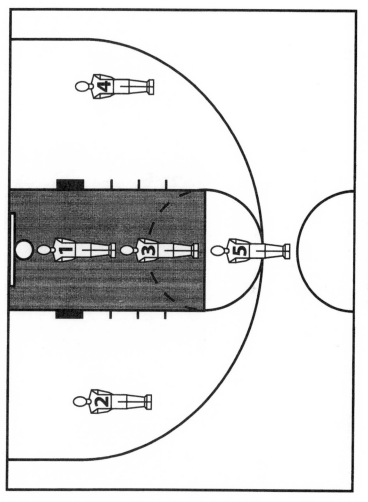

1–3–1 zone defense

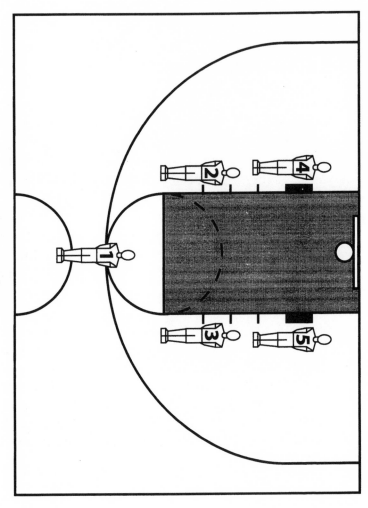

1–2–2 zone defense

the last number refers to the number closest to the basket. Obviously, in 1–3–1 and 1–2–2, the middle numbers refer to the number of defenders midway between the perimeter and the basket.

THE FULL-COURT PRESS

In most basketball games, when the offensive team is throwing the ball inbounds in the backcourt, the defensive team heads to the forecourt and gets ready to play defense. But sometimes the defensive team stays in the backcourt, defending against the inbounds pass and closely guarding the offensive players.

That's called *pressing*—but it doesn't involve a steam iron. It gets its name from a type of defense known as *full-court press,* and it relies on pressuring the offensive players to turn the ball over, either through a bad pass or a steal. It's full-court because the defensive pressure begins in the backcourt rather than waiting for the offense to cross the midcourt line.

Often a team uses a full-court press near the end of a close game, hoping to regain possession of the ball without giving the other team a chance to score. But it's hard on players: it requires a lot of physical endurance for both defensive and offensive players to be able to handle a full-court press. That's why most coaches use it only in special situations.

D Is for Defense

It isn't as pretty as a fadeaway jump shot, or as dramatic as a fast-break dunk, but defense is the key to every great team's game strategy. It doesn't matter whether it's a man-to-man press or 2–3 zone, a well-played defense can defeat (or at least mess up) a good offense.

Deciding what type of defense to use during a game—and whether or not to switch the defense—is your coach's job. That decision is based on the type of team you're playing against: the offensive plays it usually uses, who its best shooters are, whether the team is better inside or outside, and so on.

Your job as a player is to play the type of defense that your coach tells you to play. Do that well, and you'll be a valuable player to your team—and a threat to every other one. You'll also get plenty of playing time.

Play defense poorly, and you'll probably get well acquainted with the bench. Unless, of course, you're a great offensive player. But even then, a lack of defensive skills will hurt your team. And your teammates will get tired of having to play extra hard to make up for your poor defense—and for the extra points your opponents will probably make when they figure out that you're the weak link in the defense.

Game strategy relies as much on defense as on offense—and sometimes more. Don't think that just because you've got a sweet outside shot, that's all you need to contribute. It isn't.

When you're playing defense in a basketball game, you're trying to do two things. First, you're trying to prevent the other team from scoring. Second, you're trying to get possession of the ball. Doing either one of these things takes a combination of individual effort and teamwork.

Or, to put it more simply, you have to use both your head and your hands (as well as your feet and your mouth). Once you can do that, you'll be on your way to being a good defensive player. And you'll be half the way toward being a great basketball player.

Afterword

 ## THE LAST WORD: THE VALUE OF TEAM SPIRIT

Okay, so now you know what it takes to excel as a basketball player: physical and mental fitness, a basic knowledge of the rules, and good offensive and defensive skills. And, of course, practice, practice, practice.

But there's one more thing you need as a player that will help you play well on the court. You need to understand the importance of team spirit.

What is team spirit? It's the feeling shared by a group of players that they're all going to work together to play as well as they can every time they step foot on a basketball court. It's the sense that every game is a group effort, and that every player is ready to help every other player do well on the court—and off it. Though everyone on a team might not be close friends, they are all close teammates, combining their energy and skills toward the goal of being the best team that they can be.

Team spirit begins with understanding that basketball is a team sport—that no single player can win or lose a game, that all of the players on the floor have important roles to play on both offense and defense. Working as a unit, you and all of your teammates will be better players—and your team will be a better team. It will have spirit—and so will you.

Remember that. And remember this: Team spirit is the difference between a good basketball team and a great one.

Glossary

THERE'S A WORD FOR THAT: BASKETBALL TERMS YOU OUGHT TO KNOW

Every sport has its own special language—words and phrases that belong specifically to that sport. Basketball is filled with them. Here are some of the most important terms you ought to know.

Airball A shot that gets plenty of air time—because the ball never makes it to the hoop.

Alley-oop A shot that requires two players to perform: one to lob the ball toward the basket while the other jumps up, catches it, and dunks it—all while still in the air. This is a guaranteed crowd pleaser, when it works.

Backcourt The half of the court in which a team plays defense—it's where the opponents' basket is.

Bankshot A shot that hits the backboard before (hopefully) going into the basket.

Baseline The line at each end of the court that marks the end of the court; beyond this line, a ball or player is out of bounds.

Box out When a player gets between his or her opponent and the basket in an attempt to snag a rebound.

Brick A shot that not only misses the mark, rocketing off the rim or banging off the backboard, but that looks bad doing it, too.

Center   The position on a basketball team usually played by the tallest player. It's the center of the action, involving scoring in the lane with layups, hook shots, and short jumpers, pulling down rebounds, and blocking shots.

Charge   A type of foul caused by an offensive player running into a defensive player who's not moving.

Cut   A speedy move by an offensive player who's trying to get away from a defender and score off the dribble or off a pass from a teammate.

Defense   The team that doesn't have the ball—and that's trying to prevent the other team from scoring a basket.

Double dribble   A violation called when a player bounces the ball, stops bouncing it, then starts again—or touches the ball with both hands while bouncing it. Neither is permitted. The result is that the team that had the ball turns it over to the other team.

Dribble   Bouncing the ball with one hand at a time while either standing still or moving on the basketball court.

Dunk   A shot that involves jumping into the air and jamming the ball into the basket, usually to the sound of fans applauding wildly and yelling things like, "That's what I'm talkin' about!" and "In your face!"

Elbow   The area of a basketball court on either end of the free throw line.

Fast break   A play that happens when the team on defense pulls down a rebound after the offensive team has missed a shot and rapidly moves the ball to the other end of the court, often resulting in a layup or a slam dunk.

Flagrant foul   A violation in the NBA that's called when one player deliberately elbows, knees, kicks, or shoves another player. The penalty is a free throw for the player who was fouled.

Forward   The position on a basketball team that's shared by two players, both of whom play close to the basket. Sometimes the two forwards are divided into a *power forward* who helps the center with rebounding and close-in shots, and a *small forward* who supplies both inside and outside shooting skills.

Foul A violation of the rules of the game, usually called when one player has made contact or interfered with another (a *personal foul*), or when a player or coach has broken a rule or disrespected an official (a *technical foul*). The result is one or more free throws for the opposing team.

Foul out The result of a player reaching the limit on the number of fouls allowed in a game—five in high school and college, six in the Olympics and the NBA. At that point, the player has to leave the court and sit out the rest of the game.

Free throw A shot taken from the free throw line by a player who has been fouled by an opponent. No one can try to prevent the shooter from scoring—it's a "free" shot (which hopefully isn't a "throw"). Also known as a **foul shot.**

Free throw lane This is the rectangular area in front of each basket; it's also known as the **foul lane,** or as **the paint,** because it's usually painted a different color than the rest of the floor, or as **the key,** because from above, the lane with the three-point arc at its end looks like a key.

Free throw line The line at the top of the foul lane where a player who's shooting a free throw must stand. Also known as the **foul line.**

Frontcourt The half of the court where a team plays offense when it has possession of the ball—it's where that team's basket is.

Game clock The clock that keeps track of the time left in each quarter or half of a game.

Goaltending A violation called by an official when a defensive player touches the ball as it's heading down into the basket. The result is two points (or three, if the shot was taken from beyond the three-point arc) for the offense.

Guard A position on a basketball team shared by two players, both of whom are responsible for taking outside shots and running the offensive game plan. Sometimes guards are divided into a *shooting guard* who takes most of the outside shots, and a *point guard* who signals the plays and moves the ball.

Hook shot A shot in which the player with the ball faces away from the basket, pivots either right or left, raises the shooting arm overhead in a curved position, and releases the ball into a high arch, either banking it off the backboard or swishing it through the hoop.

Hoop The basket in basketball.

Hoops Another term for basketball, as in "Wanna go shoot some hoops?"

Intentional foul When one player fouls another player without trying to defend against the ball. The result is two free throws and possession of the ball by the fouled player's team.

Jump ball What a referee calls when two opponents struggle for possession of the ball. A sign on the scorer's table indicates which team gets the ball: possession alternates from one jump-ball call to the next.

Jump shot A shot taken by a player who leaps into the air before releasing the ball.

Layup A shot in which a player drives from one side of the basket and banks the ball off the backboard into the net.

Midcourt line The center line on the basketball court; it's also known as the **half-court line** or the **timeline.** Its name comes from the fact that the offensive team has ten seconds in which to get the ball from the backcourt to the forecourt: the timeline separates the two. Failing to get the ball over the line means loss of possession.

Offense   The team that has the ball and is trying to score a basket.

One-and-one   A free-throw situation in high school and college games in which a player who has been fouled shoots one free throw and has to make it to get the chance to take a second free throw. One-on-one calls happen after the team committing the foul has a total of seven team fouls (the total number of fouls committed by all of its players) in a game half.

One-on-one   A matchup between one offensive player and one defensive player, with the winner getting bragging rights (offense: "I stuffed you!" or defense: "I schooled you!").

Over-and-back   A violation called when the offensive team gets the ball across the midcourt line into the fore-court, then passes it back into the backcourt. The penalty is loss of possession.

Pass   The movement of the ball from player to player by throwing it, bouncing it, or tipping it.

Pivot foot   The foot that a player who has the ball must keep on the floor when not dribbling. It's the foot that serves as a hinge when the player swivels (pivots) to pass or shoot the ball.

Post   The area from the free throw line to the basket, out-side of the lane. It's where players **post up,** or stand, so they can take shots or grab rebounds. A player close in to the basket is playing the **low post;** one out by the free throw line is playing the **high post.**

Rebound   A missed shot that bounces off the basket or backboard and is grabbed by a player from either team.

Referee   The officials with whistles around their necks who are on the floor during the game, watching for fouls and rules violations, and getting yelled at by upset fans.

Screen   A block set by an offensive player that slows down or stops a defensive player from getting into position on the floor. When a screen is set to help the player with the ball, it's called a **pick.**

Shot   An attempt by an offensive player to get the ball into the basket.

Shot clock   A timekeeping device used in college and professional games; it shows the amount of time left for an offensive team to shoot the ball or lose possession.

Sideline   The markings on each side of the basketball court that separate inbounds territory from out-of-bounds territory.

Steal   When a defensive player grabs or slaps the ball away from an offensive player.

Three-pointer   A shot taken from beyond the three-point arc on the floor; also known as a **trey.**

Three-second violation   When an offensive player stands in the lane for more than three seconds.

Travel   A violation called when the player with the ball takes more than two steps, drags the pivot foot, or jumps into the air and lands again still holding the ball. The penalty is loss of possession.

Turnover   When the team with the ball loses possession by throwing the ball out of bounds, having a pass intercepted, traveling, or double dribbling.

Violation   Anything that a team does that results in loss of possession.

Wing   The area of a basketball court outside the lane and beyond the three-point arc.

Resources

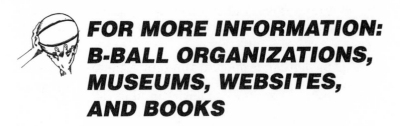

FOR MORE INFORMATION: B-BALL ORGANIZATIONS, MUSEUMS, WEBSITES, AND BOOKS

Basketball isn't just a sport anymore: it's a way of life, a passion, a reason for going somewhere on vacation. In other words, it provides players and fans access to information galore, as well as things to look at and stuff to collect that far exceeds anything James Naismith ever dreamed of when he first suggested tossing a soccer ball at a peach basket.

Here's some of what's available out there in basketball land.

ORGANIZATIONS

The Amateur Athletic Union (AAU)

The AAU has been involved in basketball practically since the beginning of the sport. It continues to play a significant role today by sanctioning thousands of teams nationwide. Some teams are affiliated with schools, churches, parks departments, or community centers. Others are independent teams that practice and play at sports clubs, fitness centers, YMCAs, YWCAs, and other sites.

AAU basketball is open to amateur athletes of all ages. For young players, there's a boys' basketball program and a girls' basketball program. The teams in the boys' program, which includes age brackets for boys from nine to nineteen years old, play by the rules of the National Federation of High Schools. The teams in the girls' program, which includes age brackets for girls from ten to eighteen years old, play by NCAA rules.

To learn about AAU teams in your area, contact the organization's national headquarters in Lake Buena Vista, Florida at 1-800-AAU-4USA, or online at **www.aausports.org.** For information specifically about the boys' program, check out **www.aauboysbasketball.org;** for the girls' program, check out **www.aaugirls basketball.org.**

YMCA/YWCA

The first basketball game ever played was at a YMCA. And Y's are still one of the best places around to find a team or a league to join—or to find a friendly pickup game. To find out what's happening in your area, contact the nearest YMCA or YWCA. You'll find telephone numbers in your local phone book, or online at **www.ymca.org** or **www.ywca.org.**

If there isn't a Y near you, try the local Boys Club, Girls Club, or churches with youth sports programs.

USA Basketball

This organization is made up of a variety of men's and women's basketball associations throughout America. It oversees the selection and training of teams that represent the United States in national and international competitions.

Based in Colorado Springs, Colorado, USA Basketball is responsible for the American teams that play in the Olympics, the World Championships, the Goodwill Games, the Pan American Games, the World University Games, and the Junior World Championships. It also sanctions foreign tours by U.S. teams, tours of the United States by foreign teams, and the certification of officials who work in national and international competitions.

To learn more about USA Basketball and its programs, check out its Website at **www.usabasketball.com** or call 719-590-4800.

Federation International de Basketball Amateur (FIBA)

Otherwise known as the International Federation for the Sport of Basketball, this organization oversees basketball competitions worldwide. With more than two hundred nations represented in its membership, FIBA is divided into five regions: Europe, Asia, the Americas, Africa, and Oceania (Australia and the South Pacific islands).

In addition to the Olympics and the Pan American Games, FIBA has such internationally famous competitions as the European Championships and the FIBA World Championship of Basketball on its list of responsibilities.

To learn more about FIBA, check out its Website at **www.fiba.com.**

National Basketball Association (NBA) and Women's National Basketball Association (WNBA)

These organizations oversee the operations of the men's professional basketball teams in the NBA, as well as the women's professional teams in the WNBA. With headquarters in New York (as well as a large retail store that sells an array of NBA and WNBA team clothing and equipment), the NBA and WNBA are the best-known professional basketball organizations in the world. To learn more, take a look at:

- **www.nba.com**   This is the official site for everything you ever want to know about the NBA, including team and player statistics, league news, pictures, links to each NBA team site, and online shopping at the NBA store.
- **www.wnba.com**   This is the official site for the WNBA, and like the NBA site it includes team and player information, league news, photos, and links to team sites.

National Wheelchair Basketball Association (NWBA)

So you think being in a wheelchair would prevent you from playing basketball? Think again. The National Wheelchair Basketball Association, which has been around since 1948, represents the thousands of wheelchair athletes who play basketball on nearly two hundred men's, women's, college, and youth teams throughout the United States and Canada.

In addition to regular-season games, the NWBA sponsors tournaments for the teams in its twenty-two conferences. Its athletes are as serious about what they're doing, and as dedicated to the sport, as any NBA player.

Wheelchair basketball is played on regulation-sized courts, but some of the rules have been changed to accommodate players' different abilities. Dribbling, for example, in a wheelchair game, a player can dribble by first giving his or her chair up to two pushes, then bouncing the ball one or more times, then pushing the chair's wheels again, and so on. Or by using one hand to wheel the chair while bouncing the ball with the other.

To learn more about wheelchair basketball, you can call the organization's headquarters in Hartford, Connecticut, at 860-525-6758, or check it out on the Web at **www.nwba.org.**

MUSEUMS AND HALLS OF FAME

The Naismith Memorial Basketball Hall of Fame

If there's one place that could be said to be the center of the basketball universe, it's the Naismith Memorial Basketball Hall of Fame in Springfield, Massachusetts. Every year more than 150,000 visitors stop by the Hall of Fame to remember great players and coaches from the past and to relive exciting moments in basketball history, from the sport's earliest days to its worldwide popularity today.

The Hall of Fame honors male and female players,

coaches, and game officials from all levels of the sport—
high school, college, professional, and international. It's
one of the best places to go when you're looking for information about, or inspiration from, past b-ballers. From
the uniform that Wilt Chamberlain wore on March 2,
1962, when he scored a hundred points in a game to the
very first twenty-four-second clock, you can find out more
about basketball history at the Hall of Fame than anywhere else.

For more information, check out the Hall of Fame's
Website at **www.hoophall.com.**

The Women's Basketball Hall of Fame

Located in Knoxville, Tennessee, the Women's Basketball Hall of Fame concentrates on significant figures
from the history of women's basketball—players (only
women) and coaches (both men and women). From a film
about that history to displays of Olympic and WNBA uniforms to hands-on activities such as dribbling and shooting, this place houses an array of things to see and do.
There's even an animatronic version of Senda Berenson,
who talks about the early days of women's basketball.

For more information, check out the Women's Basketball Hall of Fame's Website at **www.wbhof.com.**

The Indiana Basketball Hall of Fame

Many places in the United States are crazy about basketball, but no place is crazier than Indiana. The state
has turned out great players (Oscar Robertson, George
McGinnis, Larry Bird, Steve Alford) and great coaches
(John Wooden, Bobby Knight, Gene Keady, Digger

Phelps). It's home to an annual high school tournament that's the cause of "Hoosier Hysteria" (otherwise known as "outrageous fan enthusiasm").

The Indiana Basketball Hall of Fame, which is in the town of New Castle, about thirty-five miles east of Indianapolis, celebrates the state's love affair with b-ball through hands-on (and hands-off) exhibitions, films, and *Indiana Basketball History Magazine*.

To learn more, you can visit the Indiana Basketball Hall of Fame's Website at **www.hoopshall.com.**

The NCAA Hall of Champions

Devoted to a variety of sports, this museum is part of the NCAA's headquarters in downtown Indianapolis. While not focused only on basketball, it does offer some great reminders of the excitement and passion of the sport at the college level, including videotapes of past Final Fours and the voices of college coaches and former athletes talking about their experiences on the court.

For more information, check out the NCAA's Website at **www.ncaa.org,** then click on the Hall of Champions link.

WEBSITES

In addition to the Websites listed for the different organizations and museums above, there are many others devoted to the subject of basketball. Here are a few:

- **www.hoopsking.com** This is an online basketball site that provides streaming video examples of a variety of basketball skills, including dribbling, ball handling, passing, shooting, and jumping. You can also play in online basketball games.

- **www.ussportscamps.com** At this site, you'll find information about a variety of sports camps around the United States, including basketball camps for boys and girls.

- **www.hoops-scoops.net** Another online training site with tips for young basketball players, plus books, videos, trading cards, and posters.

- **www.espn.com** This site is like having a direct line into *SportsCenter* and all of the other cool ESPN shows that you like. Check here for updates on men's and women's college basketball, as well as professional b-ball news, interviews with players and coaches, and other up-to-the-minute, breaking-news sort of stuff.

- **www.gballmag.com** This is an online magazine for players and fans of girls' and young women's basketball. You get the latest news about high school, college, and WNBA players, plus you can sign up to receive a biweekly newsletter. There's a chat room, a shopping site, and a search tool to find out about basketball camps.

- **www.shophoops.com** This Website sells all things basketball, from licensed NBA and NCAA hats, jerseys, and jackets to backboards, video games, DVDs, and books. While it's got more things for adults than kids, with some help from an adult (and some patience), you can find stuff for kids, too.

- **www.basketballbooks.com** This site sells some of the best basketball books around, from biographies and autobiographies of players and coaches to books on b-ball drills and history. But these are books for adults, so you'll have to make careful choices—some of them might be more technical than what you want to read.

BOOKS

It'd be nice to say that the book you're reading right now is the only basketball book you'll ever need to read, but that's not true. Especially since there are plenty of other good basketball-related books out there, both fiction and nonfiction. Here are some you should take a look at.

Books for Kids

Novels

- ***Hoops* by Walter Dean Meyers** This is a novel about Lonnie Jackson, a seventeen-year-old star player from Harlem who gets help with his game and his life from his coach, a former professional player who was forced to quit after a scandal ruined his career.

   Meyers also has written other novels set in the world of basketball. Check out ***The Outside Shot; Slam!*** and ***Fast Sam, Cool Clyde and Stuff.***
- ***Night Hoops* by Carl Deuker** This novel tells the story of a boy named Nick who works on his basketball skills by playing nighttime games with a neighbor. When Nick's older brother gives up basketball to concentrate on playing music, Nick gets a chance to shine on the court.

- **The Moves Make the Man** by **Bruce Brooks** A novel about Jerome Foxworthy (aka "The Jayrox"), who is thirteen years old, fatherless, and the only black kid in his school. His focus is on his game: he can handle a basketball with ease. When he meets a troubled white kid named Bix, the two become buddies, both on and off the court, and Jerome learns how to put basketball into the proper perspective.
- **The Million Dollar Shot** by **Dan Gutman** This is a novel about eleven-year-old Eddie Ball, who writes a poem for a contest sponsored by a candy company and wins a chance to take a foul shot during the NBA Finals. If he makes the shot, he'll win one million dollars.

Michael Jordan

- **For the Love of the Game: Michael Jordan and Me** by **Eloise Greenfield** This is a poet's look at MJ in action—and what kids can learn from him about following their dreams and flying high.
- **Salt in His Shoes: Michael Jordan in Pursuit of a Dream** by **Deloris Jordan and Roslyn M. Jordan** This book by Michael's mother and sister tell the story of a very young MJ as he tries to make himself grow taller and become a better ball player.
- **Michael Jordan** by **Chip Lovitt.**
- **Michael Jordan: Basketball Skywalker** by **Thomas R. Raber.**
- **On the Court with Michael Jordan** by **Matt Christopher.**
- **Michael Jordan: Beyond Air** by **Philip Brooks.**
- **Michael Jordan: A Biography** by **Bill Gutman.**

Other Player Biographies

- *The Kobe Bryant Story* by **Wayne Coffey,** and *Kobe Bryant: Basketball Big Shot* by **Jeff Savage** For Kobe fans, these books tell the story of his rise from a hotshot young high school player to NBA stardom with the Los Angeles Lakers.
- *Shaquille O'Neal: Basketball Sensation* by **Bill Gutman**, and *Shaquille O'Neal: Man of Steel* by **Douglas Bradshaw** These are just two of many books you'll find on the shelves that deal with Bryant's teammate Shaq. Another is one that O'Neal wrote about himself: *Shaq Talks Back: The Uncensored Word on My Life and Winning in the NBA.*
- *Allen Iverson: Motion and Emotion* by **Mark Stewart.**
- *Allen Iverson: Star Guard* by **Stew Thornley.**
- *The Vince Carter Story* by **Doug Smith.**
- *Vince Carter: The Fire Burns Bright* by **Mark Stewart.**
- *David Robinson: NBA Super Center* by **Bill Gutman.**
- *Grant Hill: Basketball's High Flier* by **Bill Gutman.**
- *Charlie Ward: Winning by His Grace* by **Charlie Ward.**

Women Players

The popularity of women's basketball has resulted in a variety of books about women players, including:

- *Raise the Roof!: WNBA Superstars* by **Michelle Smith** A behind-the-scenes peek at such WNBA

stars as Teresa Weatherspoon, Tina Thompson, Yolanda Griffith, and Dawn Staley.
- *On the Court with Lisa Leslie* **by Matt Christopher**   A look at the life of Olympic and WNBA star Leslie.
- *Shooting Stars: The Women of Pro Basketball* **by Bill Gutman**   This book follows the women on the 1996 U.S. team, which won America's first Olympic gold medal in women's basketball, from that victory into the first year of their participation in the newly formed WNBA and the ABL.
- *The Chamique Holdsclaw Story* **by Kristi Nelson**   A biography of one of the WNBA's twenty-first-century stars.
- *She Got Game: My Personal Odyssey* **by Cynthia Cooper and Russ Pate**   A firsthand account of life as a female player by Olympian and WNBA player Cooper.
- *Inside the WNBA: A Behind the Scenes Photo Scrapbook* **by Joseph Layden, James Preller, and Joe Layden**   This is a collection of action shots of players on the court.

Basketball History

- *Greatest Moments of the NBA* **by Bruce Weber**   The title says it all.
- *A History of Basketball for Girls and Women: From Bloomers to Big Leagues* **by Joanne Lannin**   Everything you want to know about the development of women's basketball, from its earliest days to the present.

Playing the Game

- ***NBA Basketball Basics* by Mark Vancil**   This book will teach you what the pros do, how they do it, and why.
- ***Basketball* by Chris Mullen with Susanna Price and Brian Coleman**   Filled with great photos, this book is a guide to basketball's basic skills from one of the NBA's great shooters.
- ***Teresa Weatherspoon's Basketball for Girls: A Pro Superstar Teaches You the Game* by Teresa Weatherspoon, Tara Sullivan, and Kelly Whiteside**   If you want to know how to play the game, there are few people better qualified to teach you than Olympian and WNBA great Weatherspoon.

Books for Adults That Kids Might Like

The bookshelves in the adult sports sections of book stores and libraries are jammed with books about basketball. Most of them are interesting only to adults, but here are a few that you might like, too:

- ***Basketball for Dummies***   Written by former Notre Dame basketball coach Digger Phelps and *Sports Illustrated* writer John Walters, this book is chockful of great information on topics from b-ball basics, coaching, and training tips to college and professional highlights. It's fun to read, and filled with interesting tidbits about the game.
- ***The Complete Idiot's Guide to Basketball***   Written by former New York Knicks star Walt "Clyde" Frazier and sportswriter Alex Sachare, this book includes descriptions of basketball's rules and team strategies, plus insider information on NBA

legends and tips from famous coaches, and players. Like Digger Phelps's book, this one is fact filled and fun to read.

- ***The Art of Basketball***   Written by former NBA star Oscar Robertson and sportswriter Michael O'Daniel, this book introduces young players to the essential skills—dribbling, shooting, passing, rebounding, defense, and fitness. If you're serious about improving your skills, the Big O is a great teacher.

- ***The Biographical History of Basketball***   Written by sports historian Peter C. Bjarkman, this thick book is crammed with everything you'll ever want to know about everybody who ever mattered to the development of basketball, from the very beginning through the end of the 1990s. Because it's so long and filled with so much information, it's not the kind of book that you're likely to read all the way through. But it's a good book to have handy when you have a question about who did what and when.

The museums, Websites, and books listed above are just a small sampling of the basketball resources available today. For more information, do your own Internet search (with adult permission) or visit your local library. There's plenty of good stuff awaiting your discovery.